AF538839

ENCYCLOPAEDIC DICTIONARY OF INTERNATIONAL BUSINESS MANAGEMENT

ENCYCLOPAEDIC DICTIONARY OF INTERNATIONAL BUSINESS MANAGEMENT

Vol. 4

by

A.S. SUDAN

ANMOL PUBLICATIONS PVT. LTD.
NEW DELHI-110 002 (INDIA)

ANMOL PUBLICATIONS PVT. LTD.
4374/4B, Ansari Road, Daryaganj
New Delhi-110 002
Phones: 23261597, 23278000, 23255577
Email: anmolpublications@vsnl.com

Encyclopaedic Dictionary of International Business Management

First Edition 2003
ISBN 81-261-1508-4 (Set)

PRINTED IN INDIA

Published by J.L. Kumar for Anmol Publications Pvt. Ltd., New Delhi-110 002 and Printed at Mehra Offset Press, Delhi.

PREFACE

Conventionally, 'Business' is understood as a trade or profession; an industrial, commercial, or professional operation; purchase and sale of goods and services; a commercial or industrial establishment; commercial activity; volume or quantity of commercial activity; commercial policy or procedure etc. Business operations are mainly divided into—technical, commercial, financial, security, accounting and managerial activities. Till recently managerial skills had been most neglected aspect of business operations. The term 'managing' consists of various functions, main among which are—planning, organising, commanding, coordinating and controlling.

Amidst the various schools of management thought Business Management can rightly considered as an art, a science and a profession.

As is obvious from the name of the title, the present work contains judiciously selected and well explained terms covering the International Business Management in entirety. This encyclopaedic dictionary will prove a reliable asset to one and all in the field.

—A.S. Sudan

R

Fifth letter of a Nasdaq stock symbol specifying that the stock has rights.

Radar alert

Close monitoring of trading patterns in a company's stock by senior managers to uncover unusual buying activity that might signal a takeover attempt. See: Shark watcher.

Raider

Individual or corporate investor who intends to take control of a company (often ostensibly for greenmail) by buying a controlling interest in its stock and installing new management. Raiders who accumulate 5% or more of the outstanding shares in the target company must report their purchases to the SEC, the exchange of listing, and the target itself. See: takeover.

Rainmaker

A valuable employee, manager or subcontracted person who brings new business to a company.

Rally (recovery)

An upward movement of prices. Opposite of reaction.

RAM

See: Reverse-annuity mortgage.

Random variable

A function that assigns a real number to each and every possible outcome of a random experiment.

Random walk

Theory that stock price changes from day to day are accidental or haphazard; changes are independent of each other and have the same probability distribution. Many believers in the random walk theory believe that it is impossible to outperform the market consistently without taking additional risk.

Randomized strategy

A strategy of introducing into the decision-making process a chance element that is designed to confound the information content of the decision-maker's observed choices.

Range

The high and low prices, or high and low bids and offers, recorded during a specified time.

Range forward

A forward exchange rate contract that places upper and lower bounds on the future cost of foreign exchange.

Rank in Person

The personal rank that a Foreign Service officer maintains even when occupying a job of higher or lower rank.

RAP

See: Regulatory accounting procedures.

Rate anticipation swaps

An exchange of bonds in a portfolio for new bonds that will achieve the target portfolio duration, given the investor's assumptions about future changes in interest rates.

Rate base

The value of a regulated public utility and its operations as defined by its regulators and on which the company is allowed to earn a particular rate of return.

Rate covenant

A provision governing a municipal revenue project financed by a revenue bond issue, which establishes the rates to be charged users of the new facility.

Rate lock

An agreement between the mortgage banker and the loan applicant guaranteeing a specified interest rate for a designated period, usually 60 days.

Rate of Exchange

The basis upon which money of one country will be exchanged for that of another. Rates of exchange are established and quoted for foreign currencies on the basis of the demand, supply, and stability of the individual currencies. See "Exchange."

Rate of interest

The rate, as a proportion of the principal, at which interest is computed.

Rate of return

Calculated as the (value now minus value at time of purchase) divided by value at time of purchase. For equities, we often include dividends with the value now. See also: Return, annual rate of return.

Rate of return ratios

Ratios that measure the profitability of a firm in relation to various measures of investment in the firm.

Rate risk

In banking, the risk that profits may drop or losses occur because a rise in interest rates forces up the cost of funding fixed-rate loans or other fixed-rate assets.

Ratings

An evaluation of credit quality of a company's debt issue by Thomson Financial BankWatch, Moody's, S&P, and Fitch Investors Service. Investors and analysts use ratings to assess the riskness of an investment.

Rational expectations

The idea that people rationally anticipate the future and respond today to what they see ahead. This concept was pioneered by Nobel Laureate, Robert E. Lucas, Jr.

Ratio analysis

A way of expressing relationships between a firm's accounting numbers and their trends over time that analysts use to establish values and evaluate risks.

Ratio Calendar Combination

A strategy consisting of a simultaneous position of a ratio calendar spread using "calls" and a similar position using puts, where the striking price of the "calls" is greater that the striking price of the "puts".

Ratio Calendar Spread

Selling more near-term options than longer-term ones

purchased, all with the same strike; either puts or calls.

Ratio Spread

Constructed with either puts or calls, the strategy consists of buying a certain amount of options and then selling a larger quantity of more out-of-the-money options.

Ratio Strategy

A strategy in which one has an unequal number of long secruities and short sercurities. Normally, it implies a preponderance of short options over either long options or long stock.

Ratio writer

An option writer who does not own the number of shares required to cover the call options he or she writes.

Raw material

Materials a manufacturer converts into a finished product.

Raw material supply agreement

As used in connection with project financing, an agreement to furnish a specified amount per period of a specified raw material.

RE

The two-character ISO 3166 country code for REUNION.

Reachback

The ability of a tax shelter or limited partnership to deduct certain costs and expenses at the end of the year that were incurred throughout the entire year.

Reaction

A decline in prices following an advance. Opposite of rally.

Reading the tape

Judging the performance of stocks by monitoring changes in price as they are displayed on the ticker tape.

Real

Used in the context of general equities. (1) natural, (2) not dividend roll-or program trading-related; (3) not tax-related. "Real" indications have three major repercussions: a) pricing will be more favorable to the other side of the trade since an investment bank is not committing any capital; b) price pressure will be stronger if real since a natural buyer/seller may have information leading to his decision or more behind it, and c) an uptick may be required for the trader to transact if the indication is not real and the trader has no long position.

Real assets

Identifiable assets, such as land and buildings, equipment, patents, and trademarks, as distinguished from a financial investment.

Real appreciation/depreciation

A change in the purchasing power of a currency.

Real body

On a candlestick line, it is the broad part consisting of the difference between opening and closing prices.

Real capital

Wealth that can be represented in financial terms, such as savings account balances, financial securities, and real estate.

Real cash flow

Income expressed in current purchasing power terms.

Real Currency

The purchasing power in today's currency of future nominal currency to be disbursed or received.

Real Dollars

See Constant Dollars.

Real estate

A piece of land and whatever physical property is on it.

Real estate appraisal

An estimate of the value of property using various methods.

Real estate broker

An intermediary who receives a commission for arranging and facilitating the sale of a property for a buyer or a seller.

Real Estate Investment Trust (REIT)

REITs invest in real estate or loans secured by real estate and issue shares in such investments. A REIT is similar to a closed-end mutual fund.

Real Estate Mortgage Investment Conduit (REMIC)

A pass-through tax entity that can hold mortgages secured by any type of real property and can issue multiple classes of ownership interests to investors in the form of pass-through certificates, bonds, or other legal forms. A financing vehicle created under the Tax Reform Act of 1986.

Real exchange rates

Exchange rates that have been adjusted for the inflation differential between two countries.

Real gain or loss

A gain or loss adjusted for increasing prices by an inflation index such as the CPI.

Real GDP

Inflation-adjusted measure of Gross Domestic Product.

Real income

The income of an individual, group, or country adjusted for inflation.

Real interest rate

The rate of interest excluding the effect of expected inflation; that is, the rate that is earned in terms of constant-purchasing-power dollars. Interest rate expressed in terms of real goods, i.e. nominal interest rate adjusted for expected inflation.

Real market

The bid and offer prices at which a dealer could execute the desired quantity of shares. Quotes in the brokers market.

Real option

An option or option-like feature embedded in a real investment opportunity.

Real property

Land plus all other property that is in some way attached to the land.

Real rate of return

The percentage return on some investments that has been adjusted for inflation.

Real return

The actual payback on an investment after removing the effect of inflation.

Real time

A real-time stock or bond quote is one that states a security's most recent offer to sell or bid (buy). Different from a delayed quote, which shows the same bid and ask prices 15 minutes and sometimes 20 minutes after a trade takes place.

Realistic on price

In trading, and indication that the size under consideration requires price give, especially with illiquid stocks. See: Takes price.

Realized compound yield

Yield assuming that coupon payments are invested at the going market interest rate at the time of their receipt and held thus until the bond matures.

Realized profit (or loss)

A capital gain or loss on securities held in a portfolio that has become actual by the sale or other type of surrender of one or many securities.

Realized return

The return that is actually earned over a given time period.

Realized yield

The holding-period return actually generated from an investment in a bond.

Realtor

A specific designation given to members of real estate firms affiliated with the National Association of Realtors (NAR) who are trained and licensed to assist clients in buying and selling real estate.

Rebalancing

Realigning the proportions of assets in a portfolio as needed.

Rebate

Negotiated return of a portion of the interest earned by the lender of stock to a short seller. When a stock is sold short, the seller borrows stock from an owner or custodian and delivers it to the buyer. The proceeds are delivered to the lender. The borrower, who is short, often wants a rebate of the interest earned on the proceeds under the lender's control, especially when the stock can be borrowed from many sources. Note: The seller must pay the lender any dividends paid out or, in the case of bonds, interest that accrues daily during the term of the loan.

Recalculation method

A method of calculating required minimum distributions from a retirement plan using life expectancy tables. Unisex data tables allow a plan holder to determine the applicable life expectancy each year a distribution is required.

Recapitalization proposal

Often used in risk arbitrage. Plan by a target company to restructure its capitalization (debt and equity) in a way to ward off a hostile or potential suitor.

Recapture

A provision in a contract that allows one party to recover (recapture) some degree of possession of an asset, such as a share of the profits derived from some property.

Receipts

Funds collected from selling land, capital, or services, as well as collections from the public (budget receipts), such as taxes, fines, duties, and fees.

Receive fixed counterparty

The transactor in an interest rate swap who receives payments based on the fixed rate and makes payments based on the floating rate.

Receive floating counterparty

The transaction in an interest rate swap who receives payments based on the floating rate and makes payments based on the fixed rate.

Receive versus payment

An instruction that only cash will be accepted in exchange for delivery of securities.

Receivables balance fractions

The percentage of a month's sales that remains uncollected (and part of accounts receivable) at the end of succeeding months.

Receivables turnover ratio

Total operating revenues divided by average receivables. Used to measure how effectively a firm is managing its accounts receivable.

Received for Shipment Bill of Lading

A document issued by a carrier that looks like a bill of lading as evidence of receipt of goods for shipment. This type of document is issued prior to the vessel loading and is therefore not an on board bill of lading.

Receiver

A bankruptcy practitioner appointed by secured creditors to oversee the repayment of debts.

Receiver's certificate

A debt instrument issued by a receiver and serving as a lien on the property, which provides funding to continue operations or to protect assets in receivership.

Recession

A temporary downturn in economic activity, usually indicated by two consecutive quarters of a falling GDP.

Recharacterization

The reversal of a traditional IRA contribution or conversion into a Roth IRA, or vice versa.

Reciprocal Defense Procurement Memoranda of Understanding

Reciprocal memoranda of understanding (MOU) are broad bilateral umbrella MOUs that seek to reduce trade barriers on defense procurement. They usually call for the waiver of "buy national" restrictions, customs and duties to allow the contractors of the signatories to participate, on a competitive basis, in the defense procurement of the other country. These agreements were designed in the late 1970's to promote rationalization, standardization, and interoperability of defense equipment within NATO. At that time, the MOU's were also intended to reduce the large defense trade advantage the United States possessed over the European allies. The first agreements were signed in 1978.

Reciprocal marketing agreement

A strategic alliance in which two companies agree to comarket each other's products. Production rights may or may not be transferred.

Reciprocity

The reduction of a country's import duties or other trade restraints in return for comparable trade concessions from another country.

Reciprocity includes the lowering of customs duties on imports in return for tariff concessions from other countries; the negotiated reduction of a country's import duties or other trade restraints in return for similar concessions from another country. Reciprocity is a traditional principle of GATT trade negotiations that implies an approximate equality of concessions accorded and benefits received among or between participants in a negotiation. In practice this principle applies only in negotiations between developed countries. Because of the frequently wide disparity in their economic capacities and potential, the relationship between developed and developing countries is generally not one of equivalence. The concept of "relative reciprocity" has emerged to characterize the practice by developed countries to seek less than full reciprocity from developing countries in trade negotiations.

Reclamation

A claim for the right to return or the right to demand the return of a security that has been previously accepted as a result of bad delivery or other irregularities in the delivery and settlement process.

Record date

(1) Date by which a shareholder must officially own shares in order to be entitled to a dividend. For example, a firm might declare a dividend on Nov. 1, payable Dec. 1 to holders of record Nov. 15. Once a trade is executed, an investor becomes the "owner of record" on settlement, which currently takes five business days for securities and one business day for mutual funds. Stocks trade ex-dividend the fourth day before the record date, since the seller will still be the owner of record and is thus entitled to the dividend. (2) The date that determines who is entitled to payment of principal and interest due to be paid on a security. The record date for most MBS is the last day of the month, although the last day on which an MBS may be presented for the transfer is the last business day

of the month. The record dates for CMOs and asset-backed securities vary with each issue.

Recordholder

The individual or institution listed on the Corporation's books as a securityholder as of a specified record date.

Record Owner

The stockholder of record as distinguished from the beneficial owner.

Recourse

Term describing a type of loan. If a loan is with recourse, the lender has a the ability has the ability to fall back to the guarantor of the loan if the borrower fails to pay. For example, Bank A has a loan with Company X. Bank A sells the loan to Bank B with recourse. If Company X defaults, Bank B can demand Bank A fulfill the loan obligation.

Recovery

The use of depreciation of assets to offset costs; or a new period of rising securities prices after a period of declining security values.

Redemption date

The date on which a bond matures or is redeemed.

Redemption fee

A fee some mutual funds charge when an investor sells shares within a specified short period of time.

Redemption price

See: Call price

Red herring

A preliminary prospectus providing information required by the SEC. It excludes the offering price and the coupon of the new issue.

Redeemable

Eligible for redemption under the terms of an indenture.

Redemption

Repayment of a debt security or preferred stock issue, at or before maturity, at par or at a premium price.

Redemption charge

The commission a mutual fund charges an investor who is redeeming shares. For example, a 2% redemption charge (also called a back end load) on the sale of shares valued at $1000 will result in payment of $980 (or 98% of the value) to the investor. This charge may decline or be eliminated as shares are held for longer time periods.

Redemption cushion

The percentage by which the conversion value of a convertible security exceeds the redemption price (strike price).

Redemption or call

Right of the issuer to force holders on a certain date to redeem their convertibles for cash. The objective usually is to force holders to convert into common prior to the redemption deadline. Typically, an issue is not called away unless the conversion price is 15%-25% below the current level of the common. An exception might occur when an issuer's tax rate is high, and the issuer could replace it with debt securities at a lower after-tax cost.

Rediscount

To discount short-term negotiable debt instruments

for a second time, after they have been discounted with a bank.

Red-lining

Illegal discrimination in making loans, insurance coverage, or other financial services available to people or property in certain areas because of poor economic conditions, high levels of fraudulent transaction, or frequent defaults.

Reduction-Option Loan (ROL)

A hybrid of a fixed-rate and adjustable-rate mortgage. An ROL the borrower to match the current mortgage rate, which then becomes fixed for the rest of the term. This reduction is usually allowed if rates drop more than 2% in a year.

Reengineering

Reengineering changes the way work processes are carried out, to better serve the customer, client, or citizen. Reengineering is a strategy to redefine, and perhaps reduce, the business processes of an organization. Workforce reduction may be part of reengineering. Today, information technology is usually central to the reengineering of business processes. Synonyms: process management, process redesign

Reexports

For export control purposes: the shipment of U.S. origin products from one foreign destination to another. For statistical reporting purposes: exports of foreign-origin merchandise which have previously entered the United States for consumption or into Customs bonded warehouses for U.S. Foreign Trade Zones.

Reference rate

A benchmark interest rate (such as LIBOR) used to specify conditions of an interest rate swap or an interest rate agreement.

Refinancing

An extension and/or increase in amount of existing debt.

Reflation

Government monetary action that causes a reversal of deflation.

Refund

To retire existing bond issues through the sale of a new bond issue, usually to reduce the interest rate being paid.

Refundable

Eligible for refunding under the terms of a bond indenture.

Refunded bond

Also called a prerefunded bond, a bond that originally may have been issued as a general obligation or revenue bond but that is now secured by an escrow fund consisting entirely of direct U.S. government obligations that are sufficient for paying the bondholders.

Refunding

Redeeming a bond with proceeds received from issuing lower-cost debt obligations with ranking equal to or superior to the debt to be redeemed.

Refunding Escrow Deposits (REDs)

A financial instrument involving a forward purchase contract that obligates investors to buy bonds at a certain rate when issued. The future date coincides with the first optional call date on an existing high-rate bond. In the interim, investors' money is invested in secondary market Treasury bonds. The Treasuries mature around the call date on the existing bonds, providing the money to buy the new issue and redeem the old one.

Regional bank

A bank operating in a specific region of the country, taking deposits and offering loans.

Regional Check Processing Center (RCPC)

A Federal Reserve check processing operation that clears checks drawn on depository institutions located within a specified area. RCPCs expedite collection and settlement of checks within the area on an overnight basis.

Regional fund

A mutual fund that invests in a specific geographic area overseas, such as Asia or Europe.

Regional stock exchanges

Organized national securities exchanges located outside of New York City and registered with the SEC They include: the Boston, Cincinnati, Intermountain (Salt Lake City-dormant, owned by COMEX), Midwest (Chicago), Pacific (Los Angeles and San Francisco), Philadelphia (Philadelphia and Miami), and Spokane (local mining and Canadian issues, non-reporting trades) Stock Exchanges.

Register

A company is normally required to maintain records of the members (shareholders), directors and officers and secretary of the company. These records are often referred to as a register and may or may not be open to inspection by the public, dependent on the laws of the country in which the company is incorporated.

Registered bond

A bond whose issuer records ownership and interest payments. Differs from a bearer bond, which is traded without record of ownership and whose possession is the only evidence of ownership.

Registered check

A check issued and guaranteed by a bank for a customer who provides funds for payment of the check.

Registered company

A company that is listed with the SEC after submission of a required statement and compliance with disclosure requirements.

Registered competitive market maker

An NASD-registered dealer who acts as a market maker for a designated over-the-counter stock by buying and selling that stock to maintain stability.

Registered equity market maker

Member firm of the American Stock Exchange registered as a trader to make stabilizing trades for its own account in particular securities.

Registered investment adviser

SEC-registered individual or firm that substantiates completion of education and work experience in the field, and pays an annual membership fee.

Registered investment company

An investment firm which is registered with the SEC and complies with certain stated legal requirements.

Registered Office

The official address of the company to which legal documents can be sent. Often it is a requirement under company law that the registered office is within the country in which the company is incorporated.

Registered options trader

An American Stock Exchange specialist who monitors a certain group of options to help maintain a fair and orderly market.

Registered Owner

An individual or organization to whom certificates are directly issued and who, as a result, is recorded on the Corporation's securityholder records (as maintained by the transfer agent).

Registered Retirement Savings Plan (RRSP)

Tax-sheltered retirement plan for Canadian citizens, much like an American IRA.

Registered representative

A person registered with the CFTC who is employed by and solicits business for a commission house or futures commission merchant.

Registered secondary offering

A reoffering of a large block of securities, previously publicly issued, by the holder of a large portion of some corporation through an investment firm.

Registered security

Used in the context of general equities. Securities whose owner's name is recorded on the books of the issuer or the issuer's agent, called a registrar.

Registered Shares

Shares that are issued in a shareholder's name as the holder of record.

Registered trader

A member of the exchange who executes frequent trades for his or her own account.

Registrar

Financial institution appointed to record issue and ownership of company securities.

Registration

In the securities market describes process set up pursuant to the Securities Exchange Acts of 1933 and 1934 whereby securities that are to be sold to the public are reviewed by the SEC.

Registration statement

A legal document filed with the SEC to register securities for public offering that details the purpose of the proposed public offering. The statement outlines financial details, a history of the company's operations and management, and other facts of importance to potential buyers. See: Registration.

Regression

A mathematical technique used to explain and/or predict. The general form is Y = a + bX + u, where Y is the variable that we are trying to predict; X is the variable that we are using to predict Y, a is the intercept; b is the slope, and u is the regression residual. The a and b are chosen in a way to minimize the squared sum of the residuals. The ability to fit or explain is measured by the R-square.

Regression analysis

A statistical technique that can be used to estimate relationships between variables.

Regression coefficient

Term yielded by regression analysis that indicates the sensitivity of the dependent variable to a particular independent variable. See: Parameter.

Regression equation

An equation that describes the average relationship between a dependent variable and a set of explanatory variables.

Regression toward the mean

The tendency that a random variable will ultimately have a value closer to its mean value.

Regressive tax

A tax system that provides that average tax rates decrease with increases in individuals' income brackets.

Regular settlement

Transaction in which a stock contract is settled and delivered on the fifth full business day following the date of the transaction (trade date). In Japan, regular settlement occurs three business days following the trade date; in London, two weeks following the trade date (at times, three weeks); in France, once per month.

Regular way settlement

In the money and bond markets, the standard basis on which some security trades are settled is that the delivery of the securities purchased is made against payment in Fed funds on the day following the transaction.

Regulated commodities

The group of registered commodity futures and options contracts traded on organized U.S. futures exchanges.

Regulated investment company

An investment company allowed to pass capital gains, dividends, and interest earned on fund investments directly to its shareholders so that it is taxed only at the personal level, and double taxation is avoided.

Regulation A

An exemption from the Securities Act of 1933 that exempts small public offerings, valued at less than $1.5MM from most registration requirements with the SEC.

Regulation D

There are two Regulation Ds. First, it refers to the exemption from the Securities Act of 1933 for Private Placements. These placements are exempt from registration and prospectus delivery requirements. Second, it refers to a Federal Reserve Board regulation that currently requires member banks to hold reserves against their net borrowings from foreign offices of other banks over a 28-day averaging period. Regulation D has been merged with Regulation M.

Regulation FD (fair disclosure)

U.S. SEC regulation whose purpose is to ensure that select groups of investors are not privy to firm-specific information before other investors. Executives are not allowed to reveal nonpublic information during their communications with analysts and select shareholders. If information is inadvertently released, they must take steps to broaden the dissemination of the information within 24 hours of discovering the disclosure.

Regulation G

Federal Reserve Board regulation of lenders other than commercial banks, brokers, or dealers that provide credit for the purchase of or carrying of securities. This regulation was discontinued by a 1998 amendment.

Regulation M

Federal Reserve Board regulation that currently requires member banks to hold reserves against their net borrowings from their foreign branches over a 28-day averaging period. Reg M has also required member banks to hold reserves against Eurodollars lent by their foreign branches to domestic corporations for domestic purposes.

Regulation Q

Federal Reserve Board regulation imposing caps on the rates that banks may pay on savings and time deposits. Currently time deposits with a denomination of $100,000 or more are exempt from Reg Q.

Regulation T

Federal Reserve Board regulation that deals with granting credit to customers by securities brokers, dealers, and exchange member as far as initial margin requirements and securities that are covered under the rules.

Regulation T Calls

Federal Reserve Board Regulation T margin calls are issued when a customer makes a transaction in a margin account and does not meet the minimum initial requirement of 50% cash or loan available. This margin call is referred to as a Fed Call. The customer must increase the equity in the account by depositing additional funds and/or marginable securities. If the necessary amount of cash or securities is not deposited into the account within the specified time period, securities may be sold to meet the call, and the account may become restricted.

Regulation U

Federal Reserve Board limit on how much credit a bank can allow a customer for the purchase and carrying of margin securities.

Regulations

Rules specifying the appropriate behavior of agencies, organizations or individuals in the securities industry.

Regulatory accounting procedures (RAP)

Accounting principles required by the FHLB that allow S&Ls to elect annually to defer gains and losses on the sale of assets and amortize these deferrals over the average life of the asset sold.

Regulatory pricing risk

Risk that arises when insurance companies are subject to regulation of the premium rates that can they charge.

Regulatory surplus

The surplus as measured using regulatory accounting principles (RAP), which may allow the nonmarket valuation of assets or liabilities and which may be materially different from economic surplus.

Rehypothecation

Pledging to banks by securities brokers of the amount in customers' margin account as collateral for broker loans, which are used to cover margin loans to customers for margin purchases and selling short.

Reimbursement

Payment made to someone for out-of-pocket expenses has incurred.

Reinstatement

The restoration of an insurance policy after it has lapsed for nonpayment of premiums.

Reinsurance

The spreading of risk and division of client premiums among insurance companies allowing the sharing of the burden of a large risk.

Reinvestment

Use of investment income to buy additional securities. Many mutual fund companies and investment services offer the automatic reinvestment of dividends and capital gains distributions as an option investors.

Reinvestment date

The date on which an investment's dividend or capital gains income is reinvested, if requested by the shareholder, to purchase additional shares. Also known as the ex-dividend date.

Reinvestment effect

The impact of a change in interest rates on the reinvestment rate.

Reinvestment privilege

A shareholder's right to reinvest dividends and buy more shares in the corporation or mutual fund.

Reinvestment rate

The rate at which an investor assumes interest payments made on a debt security can be reinvested over the life of that security.

Reinvestment risk

The risk that proceeds received in the future may have to be reinvested at a lower potential interest rate.

Reinvoicing center

A central financial subsidiary an MNC uses to reduce transaction exposure by billing all home country exports in the home currency and reinvoicing to each operating affiliate in that affiliate's local currency. It can also be used as a netting center.

REIT

See: Real Estate Investment Trust.

Rejection

Refusal by a bank to grant credit, usually because of the applicants financial history, or refusal to accept a security presented to complete a trade, usually because of a lack of proper endorsements or violation of rules of a firm.

Relative form of purchasing power parity

Theory that the rate of change in the prices of products should be somewhat similar, but not absolutely the same when measured in a common currency, as long as transportation costs and trade barriers are unchanged.

Relative purchasing power parity (RPPP)

Idea that the rate of change in the price level of commodities in one country relative to the price level in another determines the rate of change of the exchange rate between the two countries' currencies.

Relative strength

Movement of a stock price over the past year as compared to a market index (like the S&P 500). A value below 1.0 means the stock shows relative weakness in price movement (underperformed the market); a value above 1.0 means the stock shows relative strength over the one-year period. Equation for Relative Strength: [current stock price/year-ago stock price] divided by [current S&P 500/year-ago S&P 500]. Note this can be a misleading indicator of performance because it does not take risk into account.

Relative value

The attractiveness measured in terms of risk, liquidity, and return of one instrument relative to another, or, for a given instrument, of one maturity relative to another.

Relative yield spread

The ratio of the yield spread to the yield level. Used for bonds.

Release

Relieve party to a trade of any previously made obligation concerning that trade, hence allowing the would-be transactor to show the inquiry/order to a new broker.

Release clause

A mortgage provision that releases a pledged asset after a certain portion of the total payments has been made.

Reload Stock Option

A replacement stock option granted by some companies to optionees upon a stock swap. The number of reload shares granted is equal to the number of shares delivered to exercise the option plus, in some cases, any shares withheld for tax withholding obligations. The exercise price of the new option is the current market price. The option generally expires on the same date that the original option would have.

Remainderman

One who receives the principal of a trust when it is dissolved.

Remaining maturity

The length of time remaining until a bond comes due

Remaining principal balance

The amount of principal dollars remaining to be paid under a mortgage as of a given time.

Remargining

Putting up additional cash or securities after a margin call on a brokerage customer's margin account so that it meets minimum maintenance requirements.

Rembrandt market

The foreign market in the Netherlands.

REMIC

See: Real Estate Mortgage Investment Conduit.

Remit

To pay for purchases by cash, check, or electronic transfer.

Remitting Bank

The bank that sends the draft to the overseas bank for collection.

Remote disbursement

Technique that involves writing checks drawn on banks in remote locations so as to maximize disbursement float.

Renegotiable rate

A type of variable rate involving a renewable short-term "balloon" note. The interest rate on the loan is generally fixed during the term of the note, but when the balloon comes due, the lender may refinance it at a higher rate. In order for the loan to be fully amortized, periodic refinancing may be necessary.

Renewal

Placement of a day order identical to one not completed on the previous day.

Renewable term life insurance

A policy for a stated period that may be renewed if desired at the end of the term.

Renminbi (RMB)

China's currency. The RMB is not convertible into foreign currency, and is used for internal commerce, but not in the purchase of imported goods. See also FEC (Foreign Exchange Certificate) which is a part of a two tiered china's currency system.

Rent

Regular payments to an owner for the use of some leased property.

Rental lease

See: Full-service lease.

Rent control

Municipal regulation restricting the amount of rent that a building owner can charge.

Reoffering yield

In a purchase and sale, the yield to maturity at which an underwriter offers to sell bonds to investors.

Reopen an issue

The Treasury, when it wants to sell additional securities, will occasionally sell more of an existing issue (reopen it) rather than offer a new issue.

Reopening

Treasury offerings of additional amounts of outstanding issues, rather than an entirely new issue. A reopened issue will always have the same maturity date, CUSIP number, and interest rate as the original issue.

Reorg (or Corporate Action or Reorganization)

Any transaction involving the issuance of stock or cash, or the cancellation of stock tendered by a shareholder, such as in the case of a merger, acquisition or tender offer.

Reorganization

Creation of a plan to restructure a debtor's business and restore its financial health.

Reorganization bond

A bond issued by a company undergoing a reorganization process.

Repatriation

The return from abroad of the financial assets of an organization or individual.

Replacement Chain

A concept that views a capital investment as an indefinite commitment to a specific type of technology. The replacement chain concept can be used to allow the comparison of mutually exclusive investments with unequal lives.

Replacement cost

Cost to replace a firm's assets.

Replacement cost accounting

An accounting method that includes as part of depreciation the difference between the original purchase price of an asset and the current replacement cost.

Replacement cost insurance

Insurance that pays out the full amount required to replace damaged property with new property, without taking into account the depreciated value of the property.

Replacement cycle

The frequency with which an asset is replaced by an equivalent asset.

Replacement value

Current cost of replacing the firm's assets.

Replacement-chain problem

Idea that future replacement decisions must be taken into account in selecting among projects.

Replicating portfolio

A portfolio constructed to match an index or benchmark.

Repo

An agreement in which one party sells a security to another party and agrees to repurchase it on a specified date for a specified price. See: Repurchase agreement.

Report

Written or oral confirmation that all or part of one's order has been executed, including the price and size parameters of the trade being reported; often followed by a fresh picture.

Report of Condition and Income

Financial report that all banks, bank holding companies, savings, and loan associations, Edge Act and agreement corporations, and certain other types of organizations must file with a federal regulatory agency. Informally termed a call report.

Reported factor

The pool factor as reported by the bond buyer for a given amortization period.

Reporting currency

The currency in which the parent firm prepares its own financial statements; that is, US dollars for a US company.

Repricing

To change the price of an asset. In derivatives, it sometimes refers to the exchange of options of with different strike prices.

Reproducible assets

A tangible asset with physical properties that can be matched or duplicated, such as a building or machinery.

Repurchase agreement

An agreement with a commitment by the seller (dealer) to buy a security back from the purchaser (customer) at a specified price at a designated future date. Also called a repo, it represents a collateralized short-term loan for which, where the collateral may be a Treasury security, money market instrument, federal agency security, or mortgage-backed security. From the purchaser's (customer's) perspective, the deal is reported as a reverse repo.

Repurchase of stock

Technique to pay cash to firm's shareholders that provides more preferential tax treatment for shareholders than dividends. Treasury stock is the name given to previously issued stock that has been repurchased by the firm. A repurchase is achieved through either a Dutch auction, open market, purchase, or tender offer.

Request/Offer

A negotiating approach whereby requests are submitted by a country to a trading partner identifying the concessions another seeks through negotiations. Compensating offers are similarly tabled and negotiated by delegates of the countries involved.

Required minimum distribution (RMD)

The minimum amount that the IRS requires must be withdrawn each year from all tax-advantaged retirement plans starting in the calendar year following the year in which the plan holder reaches age 70-1/2. Roth IRAs are exempt from this rule.

Required Rate of Return (RRR)

The minimum expected yield by investors require in order to select a particular investment.

Required reserves

The dollar amounts, based on reserve ratios, that banks are required to keep on deposit at a Federal Reserve Bank.

Required return

The minimum expected return you would need in order to purchase an asset, that is, to make the investment.

Required yield

Generally referring to bonds; the yield required by the marketplace to match available expected returns for financial instruments with comparable risk.

Requirement Contract

A purchase agreement for goods, equipment or services, the quantity or amount of which is based upon the actual needs or requirement of the agency.

Requisition Time Schedule (RTS)

A schedule issued by the State Purchasing Bureau which designates the dates that requisition for various categories of purchase will be required during the calendar year.

Rescaled Range (R/S) Analysis

The analysis developed by H.E. Hurst to determine long-memory effects and fractional Brownian motion. Rescaled range analysis measures how the distance covered by a particle increases as we look at longer and longer time scales. For Brownian motion, the distance covered increases with the square root of time. A series which increases at a different rate is not random. See: Anti-persistence, Fractional Brownian Motion, Hurst Exponent, Persistence, Joseph Effect, Noah Effect.

Rescheduled loans

Bank loans that are usually altered to have longer maturities in order to assist the borrower in making the necessary repayments.

Rescind

To cancel a contract because of misrepresentation, fraud, or illegal procedure.

Research and development (R"D)

Development of new products and services by a company in order to obtain a competitive advantage.

Research and development limited partnership

A partnership whose investors put up money to finance new product R&D in return for profits generated from the products.

Research department

The office in an institutional investing organizations that analyzes markets and securities.

Research portable

Service offered to clients that transmits investment bank research electronically by computers.

Reservation price

The price below or above which a seller or purchaser is unwilling to go.

Reserve

An accounting entry that properly reflects contingent liabilities.

Reserve currency

A foreign currency held by a central bank or monetary authority for the purposes of exchange intervention and the settlement of intergovernmental claims.

Reserve ratios

Specified percentages of deposits, established by the Federal Reserve Board, that banks must keep in a noninterest-bearing account at one of the twelve Federal Reserve Banks.

Reserve requirements

The percentage of different types of deposits that member banks are required to hold on deposit at the Fed.

Reserve Tranche

Member countries of the International Monetary Fund (IMF) have a reserve tranche position to the extent that their quotas exceed the IMF's holdings of its currency in the General Resources Account, excluding holdings arising out of purchases made by the member under all policies on the use of the IMF's general resources. A member may purchase up to the full amount of its reserve tranche at any time, subject only to the requirement of balance of payments need. A reserve tranche position does not constitute a use of IMF credit and is not subject to charges or to an expectation or obligation to repurchase. See: International Monetary Fund.

Reset bonds

Bonds that allow the initial interest rates to be adjusted on specific dates in order that the bonds trade at the value they had when they were issued.

Reset frequency

The frequency with which the floating rate changes.

Residence

Or Domicile. These are complex concepts regarding where a company or individual are considered to be located for the purposes of taxation, immigration and the application of law. 'Migration of Domicile' refers to the ability to move (a company) from one jurisdiction (country) to another.

Residential mortgage

Mortgage on a residential property, tax-deductible for individuals up to $1 million.

Residential property

Property that consists of homes, apartments, townhouses, and condominiums.

Residual assets

Assets that remain after sufficient assets are dedicated to meet all senior debtholders' claims in full.

Residual claim

Related: Equity claim.

Residual dividend approach

An approach that suggests that a firm pay dividends if and only if acceptable investment opportunities for those funds are currently unavailable.

Residual method

A method of allocating the purchase price for the acquisition of another firm among the acquired assets.

Residual Restrictions

Quantitative restrictions that have been maintained by governments before they became contracting parties to GATT and, hence, permissible under the GATT "grandfather clause." Most of the residual restrictions still in effect are maintained by developed countries against the imports of agricultural products.

Residual Return

Return independent of the benchmark. The residual return is the return relative to beta times the benchmark return. To be exact, an asset's residual return equals its excess return minus beta times the benchmark excess return.

Residual risk

Related: Unsystematic risk.

Residuals

(1) Part of stock returns not explained by the explanatory variable (the market index return). Residuals measure the impact of firm-specific events during a particular period. (2) Remainder cash flows generated by pool collateral and those needed to fund bonds supported by the collateral.

Residual value

Usually refers to the value of a lessor's property at the time the lease expires.

Resiliency

Speed with which new orders respond to a change in prices.

Resistance

An effective upper bound on prices achieved because of many willing sellers at that price level.

Resistance level

A price level above which it is supposedly difficult for a security or market to rise. Price ceiling at which technical analysts note persistent selling of a commodity or security. Antithesis of support level.

Resolution

A document that records a decision or action by a board of directors, or a bond resolution by a government entity authorizing a bond issue.

Resolution Funding Corporation (RefCorp)

A government agency established by Congress in 1989 to issue bailout bonds and raise funds for the activities of the Resolution Trust Corporation, as well as to administer struggling institutions inherited from the disbanded Federal Savings and Loan Corporation.

Resolution Trust Corporation (RTC)

A government agency established in 1989 and disbanded in 1996 that administered federal savings and loan institutions that were insolvent between 1989 and August 1992 by either bailing them out or merging them.

Restricted

Placed on a list that dictates that the trader may not maintain positions, solicit business, or provide indications in a stock, but may serve as broker in agency trades after being properly cleared. Traders are so restricted due to investment bank involvement with the company on nonpublic activity (i.e., mergers and acquisitions defense), affiliate ownership, or underwriting activities; signified on the Quotron by a flashing "R." A restricted list and the stocks on it should never be conveyed to anyone outside of the trading areas, much less outside the firm. See: Grey list.

Restricted account

A margin account without enough equity to meet the initial margin requirement that is restricted from any purchases until the requirement is fulfilled.

Restricted Securities

The term used under Rule 144 for securities issued privately by the company, without the benefit of a registration statement. Restricted securities are subject to a holding period before they can be sold under Rule 144.

Restricted surplus

A portion of retained earnings not allowed by law to be used for the payment of dividends.

Restricted stock

Stock that must be traded in compliance with special SEC regulations concerning its purchase and resale. These restrictions generally result from affiliate ownership, M&A activity, and underwriting activity.

Restricted Stock Award

Grants of shares of stock subject to restrictions on sale and risk of forfeiture until vested by continued employment. Restricted stock typically vests in increments over a period of several years. Dividends or dividend equivalent rights may be paid, and award holders may have voting rights, during the restricted period.

Restrictive Business Practices

Actions in the private sector, such as collusion among the largest international suppliers, designed to restrict competition so as to keep prices relatively high.

Restrictive covenants

Provisions that place constraints on the operations of borrowers, such as restrictions on working capital, fixed assets, future borrowing, and payment of dividends.

Restrictive endorsement

An endorsement signature on the back of a check that specifies the conditions under which the check can be transferred or paid out.

Restrictive Specification

Specifications that unnecessarily limit competition.

Restructuring

The reorganization of a company in order to attain greater efficiency and to adapt to new markets. Major corporate restructuring transactions include mergers, acquisitions, tender offers, leveraged buyouts, divestitures, spin-offs, equity carve-outs, liquidations and reorganizations.

Resyndication limited partnership

The sale of existing properties to new limited partners, so that they can receive the tax advantages that are no longer available to the old partners.

Retail

Individual and institutional customers as opposed to dealers and brokers.

Retail credit

Credit granted by a firm to consumers for the purchase of goods or services. See: consumer credit.

Retail house

A brokerage firm that caters to individual customers rather than large institutions.

Retail investors

Small individual investors who commit capital for their personal account rather than on behalf of another company.

Retail price

The total price charged for a product sold to a customer, which includes the manufacturer's cost plus a retail markup.

Retained earnings

Accounting earnings that are retained by the firm for reinvestment in its operations; earnings that are not paid out as dividends.

Retained earnings statement

A statement of all transactions affecting the balance of a company's retained earnings account.

Retaliation

Action taken by a country whose exports are adversely affected by the raising of tariffs or other trade restricting measures by another country. The GATT permits an adversely affected contracting party (CP) to impose limited restraints on imports from another CP that has raised its trade barriers (after consultations with countries whose trade might be affected). In theory, the volume of trade affected by such retaliatory measures should approximate the value of trade affected by the precipitating change in import protection.

Retention

The number of units allocated to an underwriting syndicate member less the units held back by the syndicate manager for facilitating institutional sales and for allocation to nonmember firms.

Retention rate

The percentage of present earnings held back or retained by a corporation, or one minus the dividend payout rate. Also called the retention ratio.

Rethinking

Rethinking is both broader and more fundamental than rightsizing. Rethinking strategically identifies and refocuses the core mission. Rethinking asks, for example: Why do we exist at all? What is our mission? Is it still the right mission? Is it still worth doing? Rethinking also asks: Assuming we should still exist, how should we go about our mission? What are our performance capacities? What redesign is relevant to the core mission? Rethinking is necessary and appropriate in periods of the greatest change. Antonym: repair

Retire

To extinguish a security, as in paying off a debt.

Retirement

Removal from circulation of stock or bonds that have been reacquired or redeemed.

Retirement Protection Act of 1994

Legislation designed to protect the pension benefits of workers and retirees by increasing required support of pension plans by employers.

Retracement

A price movement in the opposite direction of the previous trend.

Return

The change in the value of a portfolio over an evaluation period, including any distributions made from the portfolio during that period.

Returned Without Action

For export control purposes: the return of a license application without action is used when the application is incomplete, additional information is required, or the product is eligible for a General License.

Return if Exercised

The return that a covered call writer would make if the underlying stock were called away.

Return of capital

A cash distribution resulting from the sale of a capital asset, or securities, or tax breaks from depreciation.

Return on assets (ROA)

Indicator of profitability. Determined by dividing net income for the past 12 months by total average assets. Result is shown as a percentage. ROA can be decomposed into return on sales (net income/sales) multiplied by asset utilization (sales/assets).

Return on capital employed (ROCE)

Indicator of profitability of the firm's capital investments. Determined by dividing Earnings Before Interest and Taxes by (capital employed plus short-term loans minus intangible assets). The idea is that this ratio should at least be greater than the cost of borrowing.

Return on equity (ROE)

Indicator of profitability. Determined by dividing net income for the past 12 months by common stockholder equity (adjusted for stock splits). Result is shown as a percentage. Investors use ROE as a measure of how a company is using its money. ROE may be decomposed into return on assets (ROA) multiplied by financial leverage (total assets/total equity).

Return on investment (ROI)

Generally, book income as a proportion of net book value.

Return on sales

A measurement of operational efficiency equaling net pre-tax profits divided by net sales expressed as a percentage.

Return on total assets

The ratio of earnings available to common stockholders to total assets.

Return-to-maturity expectations

A variant of pure expectations theory that suggests that the return an investor will realize by rolling over short-term bonds to some investment horizon will be the same as holding a zero-coupon bond with a maturity that is the same as that investment horizon.

Reuters

International news and quotation service based in London.

Revaluation

An increase in the foreign exchange value of a currency that is pegged to other currencies or gold.

Reversal Arbitrage

A riskless arbitrage that involves selling the stock short, writing a put, and buying a call. The options have the same terms.

Revenue Anticipation Note (RAN)

A short-term municipal debt issue that will be repaid with anticipated revenues, such as sales taxes, from the project.

Revenue bond

A bond issued by a municipality to finance either a project or an enterprise in which the issuer pledges to the bondholders the revenues generated by the operation of the projects financed. Examples are hospital revenue bonds and sewer revenue bonds.

Revenue fund

A fund accounting for all revenues from an enterprise financed by a municipal revenue bond.

Revenue Reconciliation Act of 1993

Legislation created to reduce the federal budget deficit by cutting spending and increasing taxes.

Revenue sharing

The percentage split between the general partner and limited partners of profits and losses resulting from the operation of the involved business.

Reversal

Turn, unwind. For convertible reversal, selling a convertible and buying the underlying common, usually effected by an arbitrageur. For market reversal, change in direction in the stock or commodity futures markets, as charted by technical analysts in trading ranges. For options reversal, closing the positions of each aspect of an options spread or combination strategy.

Reverse-annuity mortgages (RAM)

Bank loan for an amount equal to a percentage of the appraisal value of the home. The loan is then paid to the homeowner in the form of an annuity.

Reverse a swap

Reswap of bonds to gain the advantage of a yield spread or tax loss and restore a bond portfolio to its position before the original swap.

Reverse conversion

A technique in which brokerage firms earn interest on the stocks they hold for their customers by selling the short and investing the proceeds in money market accounts. The short positions are hedged to protect against adverse market conditions.

Reverse leverage

Occurs when the interest on borrowings exceeds the return on investment of the funds that were borrowed.

Reverse leveraged buyout

Bringing back into publicly traded status a company that had been privatized by way of a leveraged buyout.

Reverse mortgage

A mortgage agreement allowing a homeowner to borrow against home equity and receive tax-free payments until the total principal and interest reach the credit limit of equity, and the lender is either repaid in full or takes the house.

Reverse Preferences

Tariff advantages once offered by developing countries to imports from certain developed countries that granted them preferences. Reverse preferences characterized trading arrangements between the European Community and some developing countries prior to the advent of the Generalized System of Preferences (GSP) and the signing of the Lom, Convention.

Reverse price risk

A type of mortgage pipeline risk that occurs when a lender commits to sell loans to an investor at rates prevailing at the time of mortgage application but sets the note rates when the borrowers closes. The lender is thus exposed to the risk of falling rates.

Reverse repo

In essence, refers to a repurchase agreement. From the customer's perspective, the customer provides a collateralized loan to the seller.

Reverse stock split

A proportionate decrease in the number of shares, but not the total value of shares of stock held by shareholders. Shareholders maintain the same percentage of equity as before the split. For example, a 1-for-3 split would result in stockholders owning one share for every three shares owned before the split. After the reverse split, the firm's stock price is, in this example, three times the pre-reverse split price. A firm generally institutes a reverse split to boost its stock's market price. Some think this supposedly attracts investors.

Reversing trade

Entering the opposite side of a currently held futures position to close out the position.

Revised estimate

The third estimate of GDP released about three months after the measurement period.

Revisionary trust

An irrevocable trust that becomes a revocable trust after a certain amount of time.

Revocable Letter of Credit

A letter of credit which can be cancelled or altered by the drawee (buyer) after it has been issued by the drawee's bank.

Revocable trust

A trust that may altered as many times as desired in which income-producing property passes directly to the beneficiaries at the time of the grantor's death. Since the arrangement can be altered at any time, the assets are considered part of the grantor's estate and they are taxed as such.

Revocation of Antidumping Duty Order & Termination of Suspended Investigation

An antidumping duty order may be revoked or a suspended investigation may be terminated upon application from a party to the proceeding. Ordinarily the application is considered only if there have been no sales at less than fair value for at least the two most recent years. However, the International Trade Administration may on its own initiative revoke an antidumping duty order or terminate a suspended investigation if there have not been sales at less than fair value for a period of 3 years. See: Tariff Act of 1930.

Revolving credit agreement

A legal commitment in which a bank promises to lend a customer up to a specified maximum amount during a specified period.

Revolving line of credit

A bank line of credit on which the customer pays a commitment fee and can take and repay funds at will. Normally a revolving LOC involves a firm commitment from the bank for a period of several years.

Reward-to-volatility ratio

Ratio of excess return to portfolio standard deviation.

Rich

Term for a security whose price seems too high in light of its price history.

RICO

Stands for Racketeer Influenced and Corrupt Organization Act. Legislation under/which inside traders may be convicted.

Rider

A form accompanying an insurance policy that alters the policy's terms or coverage.

Riding the yield curve

Buying long-term bonds in anticipation of capital gains as yields fall with the declining maturity of the bonds.

Riegle-Neal Interstate Banking and Branching Efficiency Act of 1994

Law permitting interstate banking in the US

Rigged market

Manipulation of prices in a market to attract buyers and sellers.

Right

Privilege granted shareholders of a corporation to subscribe to shares of a new issue of common stock before it is offered to the public. Such a right, which normally has a life of two to four weeks, is freely transferable and entitles the holder to buy the new common stock below the public offering price. See: Warrant.

Right here

Used in the context of general equities. In-line, emphasizing that this is a customer inquiry that is ready to be executed and not distant on price. See: Tight.

Right of first refusal

The right of a person or company to purchase some thing before the offering is made to others.

Right of redemption

The right to recover property that has been attached by paying off the debt .

Right of rescission

The right to void a contract without any penalty within three days as provided in the Consumer Credit Protection Act of 1968.

Rights Agreement (aka "Poison Pill")

An anti-takeover arrangement often established by a company in anticipation of a hostile takeover attempt. The company appoints a Rights Agent who will issue Rights certificates to each shareholder at the time of the takeover attempt. The shareholder may then exercise these rights to receive additional shares of stock and/or debentures, making the target company more expensive to acquire as a result of the additional shares outstanding, or the additional debt.

Rightsizing

Organization structure, however, is more than the boxes on a chart; more than the number of employees, positions, or jobs; and more than business processes (e.g., it includes formal and informal patterns of interaction that link all organizational elements toward mission accomplishment). Rightsizing can involve reducing the workforce (downsizing) as well as eliminating functions, reducing expenses, and redesigning systems and policies (e.g., to reduce costs or reduce organizational size). It can also require upsizing (increasing the workforce) in certain areas. Rightsizing eliminates unnecessary work and improves and prioritizes the most important work. It is a multifaceted attempt to reshape the total organization. Some adherents also give rightsizing a strong humanistic orientation. Synonyms: lean organization, revitalization, renewal, reinvention, total organizational performance, organizational design

Rights offering

Issuance to shareholders that allows them to purchase additional shares, usually at a discount to market price. Holdings of shareholders who do not exercise rights are usually diluted by the offering. Rights are often transferable, allowing the holder to sell them on the open market to others who may wish to exercise them. Rights offerings are particularly common to closed-end funds, which cannot otherwise issue additional common stock.

Rights-on

Shares trading with rights attached to them.

Rights of set-off

An agreement defining each party's rights should one party default on its obligation. A setoff is common in parallel loan arrangements.

Rings

Trading arenas located on the floor of an exchange in which traders execute orders. Sometimes called a pit.

"Ring the cash register"

Used in the context of general equities. "Take a profit." See: Profit taking.

Rio de Janeiro Stock Exchange (Bolsa do Rio)

Brazil's major securities market.

Rio Group

The Rio Group is a political forum of Latin American and Caribbean countries which promotes regional political, economic and social cooperation. The Group is comprised of 13 countries, including 11 permanent members: Argentina, Bolivia, Brazil, Colombia, Chile, Ecuador, Mexico, Paraguay, Peru, Uruguay and Venezuela and two rotating members which representing the Central American countries and the Caribbean nations.

Rising bottoms

Chart pattern showing an increasing trend in the daily low prices of a security or commodity.

Risk

Often defined as the standard deviation of the return on total investment. Degree of uncertainty of return on an asset. In context of asset pricing theory. See: Systematic risk.

Risk-adjusted discount rate

The rate established by adding a expected risk premium to the risk-free rate in order to determine the present value of a risky investment.

Risk-adjusted profitability

A probability used to determine a "sure" expected value (sometimes called a certainty equivalent) that would be equivalent to the actual risky expected value.

Risk-adjusted return

Often we subtract from the rate of return on an asset a rate of return from another asset that has similar risk. This gives an abnormal rate of return that shows how the asset performed over and above a benchmark asset with the same risk. We can also use the beta against the benchmark to calculate an alpha, which is also risk-adjusted performance.

Risk arbitrage

Traditionally, the simultaneous purchase of stock in a company being acquired and the sale of stock of the acquirer. Modern risk arbitrage focuses on capturing the spreads between the market value of an announced takeover target and the eventual price at which the acquirer will buy the target's shares.

Risk-averse

Describes an investor who, when faced with two investments with the same expected return but different risks, prefers the one with the lower risk.

Risk-based capital ratio

Bank requirement that there be a minimum ratio of estimated total capital to estimated risk-weighted asset.

Risk classes

Groups of projects that have approximately the same amount of risk.

Risk controlled arbitrage

A self-funding, self-hedged series of transactions that generally use mortgage securities (MBS) as the primary assets.

Risk factor

In arbitrage pricing theory or the multibeta capital asset pricing model, the set of common factors that impact returns, e.g., market return, interest rates, inflation, or industrial production.

Risk-Free Interest Rate

Describes return available to an investor in a security somehow guaranteed to produce that return. The risk-free interest rate compensates the investor for the temporary sacrifice of consumption.

Risk indexes

Categories of risk used to calculate fundamental beta, including (1) market variability, (2) earnings variability, (3) low valuation, (4) immaturity and smallness, (5) growth orientation, and (6) financial risk.

Risk profile

The slope of a line graphed according to the value of an underlying asset on the x-axis and the value of a position exposed to risk in the underlying asset on the y-axis. Also used with changes in value. See: Payoff profile.

Risk-return trade-off

The tendency for potential risk to vary directly with potential return, so that the more risk involved, the greater the potential return, and vice versa.

Risk tolerance

An investor's ability or willingness to accept declines in the prices of investments while waiting for them to increase in value.

Riskless arbitrage

The simultaneous purchase and sale of the same asset to yield a profit.

Riskless or risk-free asset

An asset whose future return is known today with certainty. The risk-free asset is commonly defined as short-term obligations of the US government.

Riskless rate

The rate earned on a riskless investment, typically the rate earned on the 90-day US Treasury Bill.

Riskless rate of return

The rate earned on a riskless asset.

Riskless transaction

A transaction that is guaranteed a profit, such as the arbitrage of a temporary differential between commodity prices in two different markets. The evaluation of whether dealer markups and markdowns in OTC transactions are reasonable. According to NASD, markups or markdowns should not exceed 5%.

Risk lover

A person willing to accept lower expected returns on prospects with higher amounts of risk.

Risk management

The process of identifying and evaluating risks and selecting and managing techniques to adapt to risk exposures.

Risk-neutral

Insensitive to risk.

Risk-prone

Willing to pay money to assume risk from others.

Risk premium

The reward for holding the risky equity market portfolio rather than the risk-free asset. The spread between Treasury and non-Treasury bonds of comparable maturity.

Risk premium approach

A common approach for tactical asset allocation to determine the relative valuation of asset classes based on expected returns.

Risk profile

A mapping of the change in value or profits and losses to which an organization has exposure.

Risk-return tradeoff

The basic concept that higher expected returns accompany greater risk, and vice versa.

Risk-reward ratio

Relationship of substantial reward corresponding to the amount of risk taken; mathematically represented by dividing the expected return by the standard deviation.

Risk seeker

Investor who likes to take risk and is even willing to pay for it. Also called risk lover.

Risk transfer

The shifting of risk through insurance or securitization of debt because of risk aversion.

Risky asset

An asset whose future return is uncertain.

Risk-adjusted return

Return earned on an asset normalized for the amount of risk associated with that asset.

Risk-free asset

An asset whose future normal return is known today with certainty.

Risk-free rate

The rate earned on a riskless asset.

RO

The two-character ISO 3166 country code for ROMANIA.

ROA

See: Return on assets.

Road show

A promotional presentation by an issuer of securities to potential buyers about the desirable qualities of the investments.

ROCE

See: Return on capital employed.

Rocket scientist

An employee of an investment firm (often having a Ph.D. in physics or mathematics) that works on highly mathmatic models of derivative pricing.

ROE

See: Return on equity.

ROI

See: Return on investment.

ROL

The ISO 4217 currency code for the Romanian Leu.

Rollback

Rollback refers to an agreement among Uruguay Round participants to dismantle all trade-restrictive or distorting measures that are inconsistent with the provisions of the GATT. Measures subject to rollback would be phased out or brought into conformity within an agreed timeframe, no later than by the formal completion of the negotiations. The rollback agreement is accompanied by a commitment to "standstill" on existing trade-restrictive measures. Rollback is also used as a reference to the imposition of quantitative restrictions at levels less than those occurring in the present. See: Standstill.

Roll down

To move to an option position with a lower exercise price.

Roll forward

To move to an option position with a later expiration date.

Roll, Richard

Author of path-breaking work on asset pricing including the famous Roll critique. Finance professor at UCLA.

Roll order

(1) Dividend roll; (2) Replacement of a maturing position with an identical one in the new maturity; (3) Recognizition of capital gain or loss while reestablishing the position at the risk of the market.

Roll over

To reinvest funds received from a maturing security in a new issue of the same or a similar security.

Roll up

To move to an option position with a higher exercise price. In venture capital, refers to the venture capitalist forcing small firms to merge operations in order to reduce costs

Rolling of Futures

As financial futures have short-term maturities, often 3-9 months, before or at maturity, the future must be sold and a new future (for the same asset but with a new maturity) must be repurchased.

Rollover

Means that a loan is periodically repriced at an agreed spread over the appropriate, currently prevailing rate. Most term loans in the Euromarket are made on a rollover basis as to current LIBOR rate.

Rollover IRA

A traditional individual retirement account holding money from a qualified plan or 403(b) plan. These assets, as long as they are not mixed with other contributions, can later be rolled over to another qualified plan or 403(b) plan. Also known as a conduit IRA.

Roll's Critique

That the CAPM holds by construction when performance is measured against a mean-variance efficient index; otherwise, it holds not at all. Attributable to Richard Roll in 1977.

Ross, Stephen

Developer of the Arbitrage Pricing Theory. Finance professor at MIT.

Rotation

An active asset management strategy that tactically overweighted and underweighted certain sectors, depending on expected performance. Sometimes called sector rotation.

Roth IRA

Individual Retirement Account that allows contributors to make annual contributions and to withdraw the principal and earnings tax-free under certain conditions. Maximum annual contributions are $3,000 per year (phasing up to $4,000 per year in 2005 and $5,000 per year in 2008.

Round lot

A trading order typically of 100 shares of a stock or some multiple of 100. Related: odd lot.

Rounds

Cycles of multilateral trade negotiations under GATT, culminating in simultaneous agreements among participating countries to reduce tariff and non-tariff trade barriers.

— 1st Round: 1947, Geneva (creation of the GATT)
— 2nd Round: 1949, Annecy, France (tariff reduction)
— 3rd Round: 1951, Torquay, England (accession & tariff reduction)
— 4th Round: 1956, Geneva (accession and tariff reduction)
— 5th Round: 1960-62, Geneva ("Dillon" Round; revision of GATT; addition of more countries)
— 6th Round: 1964-67, Geneva ("Kennedy" Round)
— 7th Round: 1973-79, Geneva ("Tokyo" Round)
— 8th Round: 1986-93, Geneva ("Uruguay" Round)

Round-trip trade

The purchase and sale of a security within a short period of time.

Round-trip transactions costs

Costs of completing a transaction, including commissions, market impact costs, and taxes.

Round-turn

Procedure by which the long or short position of an individual is offset by an opposite transaction or by accepting or making delivery of the actual financial instrument or physical commodity.

Royalty

Payment for the right to use intellectual property or natural resources.

RPPP

See: Relative purchasing power parity.

R square (R^2)

Square of the correlation coefficient. The proportion of the variability in one series that can be explained by the variability of one or more other series a regression model. A measure of the quality of fit. 100% R-square means perfect predictability.

RTS

See Requisition Time Schedule.

RU

The two-character ISO 3166 country code for RUSSIAN FEDERATION.

RUB

The ISO 4217 currency code for the Russian Rouble.

Rubber check

A check that bounces for lack of funds.

Rule 1Ob-5

An SEC rule that prohibits trading by insiders on material nonpublic information. This is also the rule under which a company may be sued for false or misleading disclosure.

Rule 13-d

Often used in risk arbitrage. Requirement under Section 13-d of the Securities Act of 1934 that a form must be filed with the SEC within ten business days of acquiring direct or beneficial ownership of 5% or more of any class of equity securities in a publicly held corporation. The purchaser of such stock must also file a 13-d with the stock exchange on which the shares are listed (if any) and the company itself. Required information includes the way the shares were acquired, the purchaser's background, and future plans regarding the target company. The law is designed to protect against insidious takeover attempts and to keep the investing public aware of information that could affect the price of their stock. See: Williams Act.

Rule 14-d

Often used in risk arbitrage. Regulations and restrictions covering public tender offers and related disclosure requirements.

Rule 144

Restricts solicitation of buyers to complete the sell order of an insider (unless the firm is already a buyer); signified by a flashing "E" on Quotron.

Rule 144a

SEC rule allowing qualified institutional buyers to buy and trade unregistered securities.

Rule 405

NYSE codification of "know your customer" rules, which require that a customer's situation is suitable for any investment being made.

Rule 415

Permits corporations to file a registration for securities they intend to issue in the future when market conditions are favorable. See: Shelf registration.

Rule of Absolute Priority

A condition of bankruptcy proceedings under which junior (subordinated) claim holders can receive no payment until senior (priority) claim holders are paid in full.

Rule of 72

A formula used to determine the amount of time it will take for invested money to double at a given compound interest rate, which is 72 divided by the interest rate.

Rules of fair practice

Rules established by the NASD that lay down guidelines for just and equitable principles of trade and business in securities markets.

Rumortrage

A term combining the words "rumor" and arbitrage, used to describe trading that occurs on the basis of rumors of a takeover.

Rump

Usually used in the context of a merger or acquisition. A group of shareholders who refuse to tender their shares for a merger or acquisition. In a merger of Company A and Company B for example, if a sufficient number of Company B shareholders do not tender their shares, the new company will not be able to access the cash flows of Company B.

Run

A run consists of a series of bid and offer quotes for different securities or maturities. Dealers give and ask for runs from each other.

Rundown

A summary of the amount and prices of a serial bond issue that is still available for purchase.

Running ahead

The illegal practice of trading in a security for a broker's personal account before placing an order for the same security for a customer.

Runoff

Used for listed equity securities. Series of trades printed on the ticker tape that occur on the NYSE before 4:00 p.m., but are not reported until afterwards due to heavy trading that makes the tape late.

Russell Indexes

US equity index widely used by pension and mutual fund investors that are weighted by market capitalization and published by the Frank Russell Company of Tacoma, Washington. For example, the Russell 3000 index includes the 3,000 largest US companies according to market capitalization.

Russell 1000

A market capitalization-weighted benchmark index made up of the 1000 highest-ranking US stocks in the Russell 3000.

Russell 2000

A market capitalization-weighted benchmark index

made up of the 2000 smallest US companies in the Russell 3000.

Russell 3000

A market capitalization-weighted benchmark index made up of the 3000 largest US stocks, which represent about 98% of the US equity market.

Russian Exchange

Russia's major securities market.

Russian Project Finance Bank

The RPFB is a new financial institution set up with the assistance of the European Community. The Bank is intended to develop efficient financial systems in Russia capable of channeling foreign and domestic investment into priority areas by providing medium and long-term financial and high quality investment banking advisory services to businesses.

Russian Trading System (RTS)

An electronic system in Russia, like the Nasdaq system on which the majority of Russian equities trading is conducted.

Russian Union of Industrialists and Entrepreneurs

RUIE promotes commerical links between Western firms and Soviet defense firms. The Union, an independent agency created by the Russian Central government, consists of hundreds of major entreprises and associations.

RW

The two-character ISO 3166 country code for RWANDA.

RWF

The ISO 4217 currency code for the Rwanda Franc.

S

S

Fifth letter of a Nasdaq stock symbol specifying a beneficial interest.

SA

The two-character ISO 3166 country code for SAUDI ARABIA.

Safeguards

The General Agreement on Tariffs and Trade (GATT) permits two forms of multilateral safeguards: (a) a country's right to impose temporary import controls or other trade restrictions to prevent commercial injury to domestic industry, and (b) the corresponding right of exporters not to be deprived arbitrarily of access to markets.

Safe harbor

Often used in risk arbitrage as a form of shark repellent. A target company acquires a business so onerously regulated that it makes the target less attractive, giving it, in effect, a safe harbor.

Safe harbor lease

A lease to transfer tax benefits of ownership (depreciation and debt tax shield) from the lessee, if the lessee could not use them, to a lessor that could use them.

Safekeep

Holding by a bank of bonds and money market instruments. For a fee, the bank bank clips coupons and presents for payment at maturity.

Safety cushion

In a contingent immunization strategy, the difference between the initially available immunization level and the safety-net return.

Safety-net return

The minimum available return that will trigger an immunization strategy in a contingent immunization strategy.

SAIF

See: Savings Association Insurance Fund.

Salary

Regular wages and benefits an employee receives from an employer.

Salary freeze

A temporary halt to increases in salary due to financial difficulties experienced by a company.

Salary reduction plan

A plan allowing employees to contribute pre-tax income to a tax-deferred retirement plan.

Salary Reduction Simplified Employee Pension Plan (SARSEP)

A low-cost, no-frills version of a 401(k) employee savings plan available to companies with 25 or fewer employees. It allows employees to make pretax contributions to their IRAs through salary reduction each year. The Small Business Job Protection Act of 1996 replaced SARSEPs with SIMPLE (Savings Incentive Match Plan for Employees) plans. Existing SARSEPs were allowed to add new participants, but new plans could not be formed after December 31, 1996.

Sale

An agreement between a buyer and a seller on the price to be paid for a security, followed by delivery.

Sale and lease-back

Sale of an existing asset to a financial institution that then leases it back to the user. Related: Lease.

Sales charge

The fee charged by a mutual fund at purchase of shares, usually payable as a commission to a marketing agent, such as a financial adviser, who is thus compensated for assistance to a purchaser. It represents the difference, if any, between the share purchase price and the share net asset value.

Sales Contract

Contract between a seller and buyer for the sale of goods, services, or both.

Sales forecast

A key input to a firm's financial planning process. External sales forecasts are based on historical experience, statistical analysis, and consideration of various macroeconomic factors.

Sales literature

Material written by an institution selling a product, which informs potential buyers of the product and its benefits.

Sales load

See: Sales charge.

Sales Representative

An agent who distributes, represents, services, or sells goods on behalf of foreign sellers.

Sales tax

A percentage tax on the selling price of goods and services.

Sales-type lease

The leasing out of a firm's own equipment, such as a printing company leasing its own presses, thereby competing with an independent leasing company.

Sallie Mae

See: Student Loan Marketing Association

Salomon Brothers World Equity Index (SBWEI)

A top-down, float capitalization-weighted index used to measure the performance of fixed-income and equity markets. It includes approximately 6000 companies in 22 countries.

Salomon Brothers Non-U.S. Dollar World Government Bond Index

A benchmark index that includes institutionally traded bonds other than U.S. issues that have a fixed rate and a remaining maturity of one year or longer.

Salvage value

Scrap value of plant and equipment.

Same-Day Funds Settlement (SDFS)

A method of settlement used in trading between well-collateralized parties in good-the-same-day federal funds used by the Depository Trust Company for transactions in US government securities, short-term municipal notes, medium-term commercial paper notes, CMOs, and other instruments.

Same-day substitution

Offsetting changes in a margin account during the day that result in no overall change in the balance of the account.

Samurai bond

A yen-denominated bond issued in Tokyo by a non-Japanese borrower. Related: Bulldog bond and Yankee bond.

Samurai market

The foreign market in Japan.

Sanitary Certificate

A certificate which attests to the purity or absence of disease or pests in the shipment of food products, plants, seeds, and live animals.

Santa Claus Rally

Seasonal rise in stock prices in the last week of the calendar year, between Christmas and New Year's Day.

Sao Paulo Stock Exchange

See: Bolsa de Valores de Sao Paulo.

SAR

The ISO 4217 currency code for the Saudi Arabian Riyal.

Sarbanes Oxley Act of 2002

Legislation passed largely as a result of a number of accounting scandals. Among the many features is the creation of the Public Company Accounting Oversight

Board. This board is charged to: The Board shall: 1) register public accounting firms; 2) establish, or adopt, by rule, auditing, quality control, ethics, independence, and other standards relating to the preparation of audit reports for issuers; (3) conduct inspections of accounting firms; (4) conduct investigations and disciplinary proceedings, and impose appropriate sanctions; (5) perform such other duties or functions as necessary or appropriate; (6) enforce compliance with the Act, the rules of the Board, professional standards, and the securities laws relating to the preparation and issuance of audit reports and the obligations and liabilities of accountants with respect thereto; (7) set the budget and manage the operations of the Board and the staff of the Board.

Saturday night special

Often used in risk arbitrage. Sudden attempt by one company to take over another by making a public tender offer.

SATURNS

See Structured Asset Trust Unit Repackagings.

Saucer

Technical chart pattern depicting a security whose price has reached bottom and is moving up.

Saudi Arabian Standards Organization – SASO

SASO was established in April 1972 as the sole Saudi Arabian government organization to promulgate standards and measurements in the kingdom. Primarily, SASO promulgates standards for electrical equipment and some food products. Some of these standards have been adopted by the Gulf Cooperation Council.

Savings Association Insurance Fund (SAIF)

A government organization that replaced the Federal

Savings and Loan Insurance Corporation as the provider of deposit insurance for thrift institutions.

Savings bank

An institution that primarily accepts consumer savings deposits and to make home mortgage loans.

Savings bond

A government bond issued in face value denominations from $50 to $10,000, with local and state tax-free interest and semiannually adjusted interest rates.

Savings deposits

Accounts that pay interest, typically at below-market interest rates, that do not have a specific maturity, and that usually can be withdrawn upon demand.

Savings element

Used in the context of life insurance, the cash value built up in a policy, which equals the amount of premium paid minus the cost of protection. This excess is invested by the insurance company, and the returns are tax-deferred inside the policy.

Savings Incentive Match Plan for Employees (SIMPLE) 401(k) plan

A tax-deferred retirement savings plan similar to a conventional 401(k) plan, redesigned with specific rules to meet the needs of small employers. The Small Business Job Protection Act of 1996 created these plans for companies with fewer than 100 employees. An employee's contributions are indexed for inflation, and employers must make annual matching contributions.

Savings and loan association

National- or state-chartered institution that accepts savings deposits and invests the bulk of the funds thus received in mortgages.

Savings rate

Personal savings as a percentage of disposable personal income.

SB

The two-character ISO 3166 country code for SOLOMON ISLANDS.

SBD

The ISO 4217 currency code for the Solomon Islands Dollar.

SC

The two-character ISO 3166 country code for SEYCHELLES.

Scale

Payment of different rates of interest on CDs of varying maturities. A bank is said to "post a scale." Commercial paper dealers also post scales.

Scale-enhancing

Describes a project that is in the same risk class as the whole firm. That is, the project allows the firm to grow larger in the context of their current business rather than diversify into new businesses.

Scale in

Gradually taking a position in a security or market over time.

Scale order

Order to buy (sell) a security that specifies the total amount to be bought (sold) and the amount to be bought (sold) at successively decreasing (increasing) price intervals; often placed in order to average the price.

Scaling

How the characteristics of an object change as you change the size of your measuring device. For a three dimensional object, it could be the volume of an object covered as you increase the radius of a covering sphere. In a times series, it could be the change in the amplitude of the time series as you increase the increment of time.

Scalp

To trade for small gains. Scalping normally involves establishing and liquidating a position quickly, usually within the same day.

Scalping

Buying up the good IPOs.

Scattered

Used for listed equity securities. Unconcentrated buy or sell interest.

Scenario analysis

The use of horizon analysis to project total returns under different reinvestment rates and future market yields.

Schedule B

Schedule B is a U.S. Bureau of the Census publication and is based on the Harmonized Commodity Description and Coding System (Harmonized System). Export statistics are initially collected and compiled in terms of approximately 8,000 commodity classifications in Schedule B, Statistical Classification of Domestic and Foreign Commodities Exported from the United States. See: Tariff Schedules of the United States Annotated.

Schedule C

Describes membership requirements and procedures of NASD, in its bylaws.

Schedule 13d

Disclosure form required when more than 5% of any class of equity securities in a publicly held corporation is purchased.

Scheduled cash flows

The mortgage principal and interest payments due to be paid under the terms of the mortgage, not including possible prepayments.

Scheduled Purchase

A purchase for which a bid opening date is preschedules so that agency requirements for the period covered by the contract can be gathered and combined for the Invitation for Bids.

Scope Determinations

Scope determinations deal with the product coverage of antidumping and countervailing duty orders. The Department of Commerce will determine — in response to an application from an interested party or on its own initiative — whether a certain product is included within the scope of an antidumpting and countervailing duty order.

Scorched-earth policy

Often used in risk arbitrage. Any technique a company that has become the target of a takeover attempt uses to make itself unattractive to the acquirer. For example, it may agree to sell off its crown jewels, or schedule all debt to become due immediately after a merger.

SCORE

Stands for Special Claim on Residual Equity, a certificate that entitles the owner to the capital appreciation of an underlying security, but not to the dividend income from the security.

S Corporation

A corporation that elects not to be taxed as a corporation. That is, the corporation does not directly pay federal income tax on its earnings. Similar to a partnership, it passes its income or losses and other tax items on to its shareholders.

SCR

The ISO 4217 currency code for the Seychelles Rupee.

Screen stocks

To analyze various stocks in search of stocks that meet predetermined criteria. For example, a simple value screen would sort all stocks by their price-to-book ratio and pick the stocks with the lowest ratios as candidates for the value portfolio.

Scrip

A temporary document that represents a portion of a share of stock, often issued after a stock split or spin-off.

Scripophily

Collecting stock and bond certificates for their scarcity, rather than for their value as securities.

S/D

See Sight Draft.

SD

The two-character ISO 3166 country code for SUDAN.

SDD

The ISO 4217 currency code for the Sudanese Dinar.

SDR

See: Special drawing rights.

SE

The two-character ISO 3166 country code for SWEDEN.

SEAQ

See: Stock Exchange Automated Quotation System.

Search costs

Costs associated with locating a counterparty to a trade, including explicit costs (such as advertising) and implicit costs (such as the value of time). Related: Information costs.

Seasonally adjusted

Mathematically adjusted by moderating a macroeconomic indicator (e.g., oil prices/imports) so that relative comparisons can be drawn from month to month all year.

Seasoned

In the case of equity, having gained a reputation for quality with the investing public and enjoying liquidity in the secondary market; in the case of convertibles, having traded for at least 90 days after issue in Europe, and thus available for sale legally to U.S. investors.

Seasoned datings

Extended credit for customers who order goods in periods other than peak seasons.

Seasoned issue

Issue of a security for which there is an existing market. Related: Unseasoned issue.

Seasoned new issue

A new issue of stock after the company's securities have previously been issued. A seasoned new issue of common stock can be made using a cash offer or a rights offer.

Seat

Position of membership on a securities or commodity exchange, bought and sold at market prices.

SEC

See: Securities & Exchange Commission

Secert Ballot

In the context of corporate governance, this is also known as confidential voting. An independent third party or employees sworn to secrecy are used to count proxy votes, and the management usually agrees not to look at individual proxy cards. This can help eliminate potential conflicts of interest for fiduciaries voting shares on behalf of others, or can reduce pressure by management on shareholder-employees or shareholder-partners.

SEC fee

Small fee the SEC charges to sellers of equity securities on an exchange.

Second market

The OTC market.

Second pass regression

A cross-sectional regression of portfolio returns on betas. The estimated slope is the measurement of the reward for bearing systematic risk during the period analyzed.

Second-preferred stock

Preferred stock issue that has less priority in claiming dividends and assets in liquidation than another issue of preferred stock.

Second round

Stage of venture capital financing following the start-up and first round stages and before the mezzanine level stage.

Second-to-die insurance

Insurance policy that, on the death of the spouse dying last, pays a death benefit to the heirs that is designed to cover estate taxes.

Secondary distribution/offering

Public sale of previously issued securities held by large investors, usually corporations or institutions, as distinguished from a primary distribution, where the seller is the issuing corporation. The sale is handled off the NYSE, by a securities firm or a group of firms, and the shares are usually offered at a fixed price related to the current market price of the stock.

Secondary issue

(1) Procedure for selling blocks of seasoned issues of stocks. (2) More generally, sale of already issued stock.

Secondary Offering

An IPO in which privately held shares in a corporation are sold to the public.

Secondary market

The market in which securities are traded after they are initially offered in the primary market. Most trading occurs in the secondary market. The New York Stock Exchange, as well as all other stock exchanges and the bond markets, are secondary markets. Seasoned securities are traded in the secondary market.

Secondary mortgage market

Buying and selling existing mortgage loans, which are often pooled and traded as mortgage-backed securities.

Secondary stocks

Stocks with smaller market capitalization, less quality and more risk than blue chip issues that behave differently than larger corporations' stocks.

Second mortgage lending

Loans secured by real estate previously pledged in a first mortgage.

Secretary

The Company Secretary is an officer, but not necessarily a director, of the company whose duty is to discharge the statutory obligations of the company as determined by the law applicable to companies in the jurisdiction (country) in which the company is incorporated. It is often a requirement that the secretary is a real person rather than another corporate body (company) and often there is a requirement that this person is physically resident in the country in which the company is incorporated.

Section 16(a)

Provision of the Securities Exchange Act of 1934 that requires company insiders to file periodic reports disclosing their holdings and changes in beneficial ownership of the company's equity securities.

Section 16(b)

Provision of the Securities Exchange Act of 1934 that requires that any profit realized by a company insider from the purchase and sale, or sale and purchase, of the company's equity securities within a period of less than six months must be returned to the company. It is also known as the "short-swing profit" rule.

Section 83(b) Election

A tax filing within 30 days of grant that allows employees granted stock to pay taxes on the grant date instead of on the date restrictions lapse. If an employee files the election, taxes are based on the fair market value on the grant date, with any future appreciation taxed as a capital gain. If the employee does not file an election, taxes are based on the fair market value on the date the restrictions lapse, which will be higher assuming the stock has appreciated in value.

Section 201

Section 201, the "escape clause" provision of the Trade Act of 1974, permits temporary import relief, not to exceed a maximum of eight years, to a domestic industry which is seriously injured, or threatened with serious injury, due to increased imports. Import relief, granted at the President's discretion, generally takes the form of increased tariffs or quantitative restrictions. To be eligible for section 201 relief, the International Trade Commission (ITC) must determine that: (a) the industry has been seriously injured or threatened to be injured and (b) imports have been a substantial cause (not less than any other cause) of that injury. Industries need not prove that an unfair trade practice exists, as is necessary under the anti-dumping and countervailing duty laws. However, under section 201, a greater degree of injury — "serious" injury – must be found to exist, and imports must be a "substantial" cause (defined as not less than any other cause) of that injury.

If the ITC finding is affirmative, the President's remedy may be a tariff increase, quantitative restrictions, or orderly marketing agreements. At the conclusion of any relief action, the Commission must report on the effectiveness of the relief action in facilitating the positive adjustment of the domestic industry to import competition. If the decision is made not to grant relief, the President must provide an explanation to the Congress. See: Escape clause Trade Act of 1974.

Section 232

Under section 232 of the Trade Expansion Act of 1962, as amended, Commerce determines whether articles are being imported into the U.S. in quantities or circumstances that threaten national security. Based on the investigation report, the President can adjust imports of the article(s) in question.

Commerce must report on the effects these imports have on national security and make recommendations for action or inaction within 270 days after starting an investigation. Within 90 days of the report, the President decides whether to take action to adjust imports on the basis of national security. The President must notify Congress of his decision within 30 days. See: Trade Expansion Act of 1962.

Section 301

Under section 301, firms can complain about a foreign country's trade policies or practices that are harmful to U.S. commerce. The section empowers the USTR to investigate the allegations and to negotiate the removal of any trade barriers. USTR may also self-initiate investigations. Specific timeframes for conducting the investigations are specified by law. Section 301 requires that GATT's dispute resolution process be invoked where applicable and, if negotiations fail, to retaliate within 180 days from the date that discovery of a trade agreement violation took place. See: Special 301, Super 301.

Section 337

Section 337 of the Tariff Act of 1930 requires investigations of unfair practices in import trade. Under this authority, the International Trade Commission applies U.S. statutory and common law of unfair competition to the importation of products into the United States and their sale. Section 337 prohibits unfair competition and unfair importing practices and sales of products in the U.S., when these threaten to: (a) destroy or substantially injure a domestic industry, (b) prevent the establishment of such an industry, or (c) restrain or monopolize U.S. trade and commerce. Section 337 also prohibits infringement of U.S. patents, copyrights, registered trademarks, or mask works. See: Tariff Act of 1930.

Section 416

Section 416 of the Agricultural Act of 1949 provides for the donation of food and feed commodities owned by Agriculture's Commodity Credit Corporation and is focused on people in developing countries. See: Food For Peace. Food For Progress.

Section 423

The government agency responsible for the supervision and regulation of the securities industry and markets, as well as public securities offerings and the ongoing disclosure obligations of public companies.

Section 482

US Department of Treasury regulations governing transfer prices.

Sector

Used to characterize a group of securities that are similar with respect to maturity, type, rating, industry, and/or coupon.

Sector allocation

Investment of certain proportions of a portfolio in certain sectors. See: Industry allocation.

Sector diversification

Constituting of a portfolio of stocks of companies in each major industry group.

Sector fund

A mutual fund that concentrates on a relatively narrow market sector. These funds can experience higher share price volatility than some diversified funds because sector funds are subject to common market forces specific to a given sector.

Sector rotation

An active asset management strategy certain sectors, that tactically overweights and underweights depending on expected performance. Sometimes called rotation.

Secular

Long-term time frame (10-50 years or more).

Secured bond

A bond backed by the pledge of collateral, a mortgage, or other lien, as opposed to an unsecured bond, called a debenture .

Secured debt

Debt that has first claim on specified assets in the event of default.

Securities

Paper certificates (definitive securities) or electronic records (book-entry securities) evidencing ownership of equity (stocks) or debt obligations (bonds).

Securities Act of 1933

First law designed to regulate securities markets, requiring registration of securities and disclosure.

Securities Acts Amendments of 1975

Legislation to encourage the establishment of a national market system together with a system for nationwide clearing and settlement of securities transactions.

Securities analysts

Related: Financial analysts.

Securities and commodities exchanges

Exchanges on which securities, options, and futures contracts are traded by members for their own accounts and for the accounts of customers.

Securities & Exchange Commission (SEC)

A federal agency that regulates the US financial markets. The SEC also oversees the securities industry and promotes full disclosure in order to protect the investing public against malpractice in the securities markets.

Securities and Exchange Commission Rules

Rules enacted by the SEC to assist in the regulation of US financial markets.

Securities Exchange Act of 1934

Legislation that created the SEC, outlawing dishonest practices in the trading of securities.

Securities Exchange of Thailand (SET)

The only stock market in Thailand, based in Bangkok.

Securities Industry Association (SIA)

An association of broker-dealers who sell taxable securities, which lobbies the government, records industry trends, and keeps records of broker profits.

Securities Industry Committee on Arbitration (SICA)

A private group that provides mediation services in case of customer complaints against securities firms.

Securities Investor Protection Corporation (SIPC)

A nonprofit corporation that insures customers' securities and cash held by member brokerage firms against the failure of those firms.

Securities loan

The loan of securities between brokers, often to cover a client's short sale; or a loan secured by marketable securities.

Securities markets

Organized exchanges plus over-the-counter markets in which securities are traded.

Securitization

Creating a more or less standard investment instrument such as the mortgage pass-through security, by pooling assets to back the instrument. Also refers to the replacement of nonmarketable loans and/or cash flows provided by financial intermediaries with negotiable securities issued in the public capital markets.

Security

Piece of paper that proves ownership of stocks, bonds, and other investments.

Security characteristic line

A plot on a graph of the excess return on a security over the risk-free rate as a function of the excess return on the market. The slope of this line is the security's beta.

Security deposit (initial)

Synonymous with the term margin. A cash amount that must be deposited with the broker for each contract as a guarantee of fulfillment of the futures contract. It is not considered as part payment or purchase. Related: Margin.

Security deposit (maintenance)

Related: Maintenance margin.

Security Industry Automated Corporation (SIAC)

Entity that executes automated DOT orders.

Security interest

The creditor's right to take property or a portion of property offered as security.

Security market line

Line representing the relationship between expected return and market risk or beta. The slope of this line is the risk premium for beta.

Security Market Line

The linear relationship between expected asset returns and betas posited by the Capital Asset Pricing Model.

Security market plane

A plane that shows the relationship between expected return and the beta coefficient of more than one factor.

Security ratings

Commercial rating agencies' assessment of the credit and investment risk of securities.

Security selection

See: Security selection decision.

Security selection decision

Choosing the particular stocks or bonds or other investment instruments to include in a portfolio.

SED

See: Shipper's Export Declaration.

Seed money

The first contribution by a venture capitalist toward the financing of a new business, often using a loan or purchase of convertible bonds or preferred stock. See: Mezzanine level and second round.

Seek a market

Search for a securities buyer or seller.

Segmented market

A market that is partially or wholly isolated from other markets by one or more market imperfections.

Segregation of securities

SEC rules to dictate how customers' securities may be used by broker-dealers in broker loans.

SEHK

See: Stock Exchange of Hong Kong.

Seigniorage

The profit which results from the difference between the cost of making coins and currency and the exchange value of coin and currency in the market.

SEK

The ISO 4217 currency code for the Swedish Krona.

Select ten portfolio

A unit investment trust that buys and holds for one year the ten stocks in the Dow Jones Industrial Average with the highest dividend yields.

Selective hedging

Protecting investments during some time periods and not during others.

Selected dealer agreement

The set of rules governing the selling group in an underwriting.

Self-amortizing mortgage

Mortgage whose entire principal is paid off in a specified period of time with regular interest and principal payments.

Self-directed IRA

An IRA that the account holder can after appointing a custodian manager to carry out investment instructions.

Self-employed income

Taxable income of a person involved in a sole proprietorship or other sort of free-lance work.

Self-employment tax

A tax self-employed people must pay to qualify them to receive Social Security benefits at retirement.

Self-liquidating loan

Loan to finance current assets. The sale of the current assets provides the cash to repay the loan.

Self-regulatory organization (SRO)

Organizations that enforce fair, ethical, and efficient practices in the securities and commodity futures industries, including all national securities and commodities exchanges and the NASD.

Self-selection

Consequence of a contract that induces only one group to participate.

Self-Similar

When small parts of an object are qualitatively the same, or similar to the whole object. In certain deterministic fractals, like the Sierpinski Triangle, small pieces look the same as the entire object. In random fractals, small increments of time will be statistically similar to larger increments of time. See: Fractal.

Self-supporting debt

Bonds sold to finance a project that will produce enough revenue through tolls or other charges to retire the debt . See: revenue bond.

Self Tender

A company buys back a certain percentage of its own shares through a tender offer.

Self-tender offer

A company that tenders for its own shares.

Seller financing

Funding a purchase by a seller's loan to the buyer, the buyer takes full title to the property when the loan is fully repaid.

Seller's market

Market in which demand exceeds supply. As a result, the seller can dictate the price and the.terms of sale.

Seller's option

Delayed settlement/delivery in a transaction.

Seller's points

In reference to a loan, seller's points consist of a lump sum paid by the seller to the buyer's creditor to reduce the cost of the loan to the buyer. This payment is either required by the creditor or volunteered by the seller, usually in a loan to buy real estate. Generally, one point equals one percent of the loan amount.

Sell hedge

Related: short hedge.

Selling climax

A sudden drop in security prices as sellers dump their holdings.

Selling concession

The discount underwriters offer the selling group on securities in a new issue.

Selling dividends

Inducing a prospective customer to buy shares in order to profit from a dividend scheduled in the near future.

Selling, General and Administrative (Expenses)

SGA is the sum of:

— General and administrative expenses (such as: salaries of non-sales personnel, rent, heat, and light);

— Direct selling expenses (that is, expenses that can be directly tied to the sale of a specific unit, such as: credit, warranty, and advertising expenses); and

— Indirect selling expenses (that is, expenses which cannot be directly tied to the sale of a specific unit but which are proportionally allocated to all units sold during a certain period, such as: telephone, interest, and postal charges).

Selling on the good news

A strategy of selling stock shortly after a company announces good news and the stock price rises. Investors believe that the price is as high as it can go and is on the brink of going down.

Selling group

All banks involved in selling or marketing a new issue of stock or bonds.

Selling short

Selling a stock not actually owned. If an investor thinks the price of a stock is going down, the investor could borrow the stock from a broker and sell it. Eventually, the investor must buy the stock back on the open market. For instance, you borrow 1000 shares of XYZ on July 1 and sell it for $8 per share. Then, on Aug. 1, you purchase 1000 shares of XYZ at $7 per share. You've made $1000 (less commissions and other fees) by selling short.

Selling short against the box

Selling short stock that is actually owned by the seller but held in the box, meaning it is held in safekeeping. The seller borrows securities needed to cover as the stock in the box may be inaccessible, or the seller may not wish to disclose ownership.

Selling the spread

A spread whose option to be sold is trading at a higher premium than the option to be bought.

Selling Syndicate

A group of underwriters that issues a firm's securities by buying them from the issuing firm and reselling them to a group of smaller brokerage firms for eventual sale to individual investors.

Sell limit order

Conditional trading order that indicates that a security may be sold at the designated price or higher. Related: Buy limit order.

Sell off

Sale of securities under pressure. See: Dumping.

Sell order

An order that may take many different forms by an investor to a broker to sell a particular stock, bond, option, future, mutual fund, or other holding.

Sell out

Liquidation of a margin account after a customer has failed to bring an account to a required level by producing additional equity after a margin call. The selling of securities by a broker when a customer fails to pay for them. The complete sale of all securities in a new issue.

Sell plus order

Market or limit order to sell a stated amount of stock provided that the price to be obtained is not lower than the last sale if the last sale was a plus, or zero plus tick, and is not lower than the last sale plus the minimum fractional change in the stock if the last sale was a minimum or zero minimum tick. (In a limit order, sale cannot be lower than the limit, regardless of tick.)

Sell price

See: Redemption price.

Sell-side analyst

A financial analyst who works for a brokerage firm and whose recommendations are passed on to the brokerage firm's customers. Also called a Wall Street analyst.

Sell the book

Used for listed equity securities. Order to a broker by the holder of a large quantity of shares of a security to sell all that can be absorbed at the current bid price. The term derives from the specialist's book - the record of all the buy and sell orders members have placed in the stock one handles. In this scenario, the buyers potentially include those in the specialist's book, the specialist for its own account, and broker-dealers.

Semiconductor Trade Arrangement

The U.S.-Japan Semiconductor Trade Arrangement is a bilateral agreement which came into effect on August 1, 1991, replacing the prior 1986 Semiconductor Trade Arrangement. The new Arrangement contains provisions to: (a) increase foreign access to the Japanese semiconductor market and (b) deter dumping of semiconductors by Japanese suppliers into the U.S. market, as well as in third country markets. In evaluating market access improvement, both governments agreed to pay particular attention to market share. The expectation of a 20 percent foreign market share by the end of 1992 is included in the Arrangement. The Arrangement explicitly states, however, that the 20 percent figure is not a guarantee, a ceiling, or a floor on the foreign market share.

Semistrong-form efficiency

A form of pricing efficiency that profits the price of a security fully reflects all public information (including, but not limited to, historical price and trading patterns). Compare weak-form efficiency and strong-form efficiency.

"Send it in"

Market language: "I bought your stock - 'send it in' (and possibly more)."

Senior Commercial Officer

The SCO is the senior U.S. and Foreign Commercial Officer at an embassy and reports in-country to the Ambassador. At major posts, this position carries the title of Commercial Counselor; in key posts, Minister Counselor. Usually reporting to the SCO are a Commercial Attache and Commercial officers. The latter are sometimes assigned to subordinate posts throughout the country.

Senior debt

Debt whose terms in the event of bankruptcy, require it to be repaid before subordinated debt receives any payment.

Senior mortgage bond

A bond that, in the event of bankruptcy, will be redeemed before any other bonds are repaid.

Senior refunding

Replacement by the issuer of securities with 5-to 12-year maturities with securities of 15-year or longer maturities, in order to delay, reduce, or consolidate payment.

Senior security

A security that, in the event of bankruptcy, will be redeemed before any other securities.

Seniority

The order of repayment. In the event of bankruptcy,

senior debt must be repaid before subordinated debt is repaid.

Sensitive market

A market that reacts to a great extent to good or bad news.

Sensitivity analysis

Analysis of the effect on a project's profitability of changes in sales, cost, and so on.

Sentiment indicators

The general feeling of investors about the state of the market, such as whether they are bullish or bearish.

Separate customer

Method of allocating insurance by the Securities Investor Protection Corporation. Each account that is under the name of a different person or group of people is entitled to maximum protection.

Separate tax returns

Tax returns of married persons who choose to file their returns individually, usually because this approach produces lower overall tax payments.

Separate Trading of Registered Interest and LPrincipal Securities (STRIPS)

Long-term notes and bonds divided into principal and interest-paying components, which may be transferred and sold in amounts as small as $1000. STRIPS are sold at auction at a minimum par amount, varying for each issue. The amount is an arithmetic function of the issue's interest rate.

Separation property

The property that portfolio choice can be divided into two independent tasks: (1) Determination of the optimal risky portfolio, which is a purely mathematical problem, and (2) the personal choice of the best mix of the optimal risky portfolio and the risk-free asset, which depends on a person's degree of risk aversion.

Separation theorem

Theory that the value of an investment to an individual is not dependent on consumption preferences. That is, investors will want to accept or reject the same investment projects by using the NPV rule, regardless of personal preference.

Serial bonds

Corporate bonds arranged so that specified principal amounts become due on specified dates. Related: Term bonds.

Serial covariance

The covariance between a variable and the lagged value of the variable; the same as autocorrelation.

Serial entrepreneur

Business person that successfully starts (does not kill) a number of different businesses.

Serial redemption

The redemption of a serial bond.

Series

Options: All option contracts of the same class that also have the same unit of trade, expiration date, and exercise price. Stocks: shares that have common characteristics, such as rights to ownership and voting, dividends, or par value. In the case of many foreign shares, one series may be owned only by citizens of the country in which the stock is registered.

Series bond

Bond that may be issued in several series under the same indenture document.

Series E bond

A local and state tax-free bond issued by the U.S. government from 1941 to 1979, which was then replaced by Series HH bonds.

Series EE bond

See: Savings bond.

Series HH bond

See: Savings bond.

Service charge

A component of some finance charges, such as the fee for triggering an overdraft checking account into use.

Set-aside

A percentage of a municipal or corporate bond underwriting that is allocated for handling by a minority-owned broker/dealer firm.

Set of contracts perspective

View of corporation as a set of contracting relationships among individuals who have conflicting objectives, such as shareholders or managers. The corporation is a legal construct that serves as the nexus for the contracting relationships.

Set up

Applies mainly to convertible securities. Arbitrage involving going long the convertible and short a certain percentage of the underlying common. Antithesis of Chinese hedge.

Settle price

An average of the trading prices in the futures market during the last few minutes of trading.

Settlement

When payment is made for a trade.

Settlement date

The date on which payment is made to settle a trade. For stocks traded on US exchanges, settlement is currently three business days after the trade. For mutual funds, settlement usually occurs in the US the day following the trade. In some regional markets, foreign shares may require months to settle.

Settlement options

The various possibilities open to a beneficiary under a life insurance policy as to how the benefit will be paid out.

Settlement price

A figure determined by the closing range that is used to calculate gains and losses in futures market accounts. Settlement prices are used to determine gains, losses, margin calls, and invoice prices for deliveries. Related: Closing range.

Settlement rate

The rate suggested in Financial Accounting Standards Board (FASB) 87 for discounting the obligations of a pension plan. The rate at which the pension benefits could be effectively settled if the company sponsoring the pension plan wishes to terminate its pension obligation.

Settlement risk

The risk that one party will deliver and the counterparty will not be able to pay and vice versa.

Severally but not jointly

An agreement between members of an underwriting group buy a new issue (severally), but not to assume joint liability for shares left unsold by other members.

Severance

A settlement received after being released from a corporation. In the context of corporate governance, an agreement that assures high-level executives of their postions or some compensation and are not contingent upon a change in control.

SG

The two-character ISO 3166 country code for SINGAPORE.

SGAEC

China's State General Administration of Exchange Control is responsible for currency exchange issues while the Bank of China is the only bank authorized to conduct foreign exchange business.

SGD

The ISO 4217 currency code for the Singapore Dollar.

SH

The two-character ISO 3166 country code for SAINT HELENA.

Shadow calendar

A backlog of securities issues registered with the SEC, awaiting the determination of an offer date.

Shadow stock

First, a public company may create a stock that strips out the market wide movements for the purpose of rewarding managers. That is, the management might have done a great job - but the traded stock plummets because the market as a whole plummets. A second interpretation of shadow stock is a phantom stock that is created by a private company (i.e. that does not have stock traded either on exchange or over the counter) again for the purpose of performance evaluation and rewards.

Shadows

The thin lines above and below the real body on a candlestick line.

Shakeout

A dramatic change in market conditions that forces speculators to sell their positions, often at a loss.

Sham

A business transaction, such as a limited partnership, that is entered into for the sake of avoiding tax.

Shanghai Stock Exchange

One of two major securities markets in China.

Share broker

A discount broker who charges per share traded, and reduces the per unit charge as the number of shares traded increases, as opposed to a dealer who charges a percentage of the dollar amount of the trade.

Shared Appreciation Mortgage (SAM)

A mortgage with a low rate of interest, offset by giving the lender some portion of the appreciation in the value of the underlying property.

Shared Foreign Sales Corporation

A shared FSC is a foreign sales corporation consisting of more than one and less than 25 unrelated exporters. See: Foreign Sales Corporation.

Shareholder

Person or entity that owns shares or equity in a corporation.

Shareholders' equity

This is a company's total assets minus total liabilities. A company's net worth is the same thing.

Shareholders' letter

A section of an annual report where one can find general overall discussion by management of successful and failed strategies. Provides guidance for looking at specific parts of the report.

Share repurchase

Program by which a corporation buys back its own shares in the open market. It is usually done when shares are undervalued. Since repurchase reduces the number of shares outstanding and thus increases earnings per share, it tends to elevate the market value of the remaining shares held by stockholders.

Shares

Certificates or book entries representing ownership in a corporation or similar entity.

Shares authorized

The maximum number of shares of stock of a company allowed in the articles of incorporation, which may be changed only by a shareholder vote. See: Issued and outstanding.

Shares or Stock

A company issues shares or stock to the owners of the company to designate their ownership of a portion of the company's issued capital. In many locations legislation requires the company to maintain a register of the ownership of the shares and may require this to be open to inspection by relevant authorities or by the public. Bearer shares are issued to the holder (bearer) of the shares and no record of to whom the bearer shares were issued are maintained. Thus, the ownership cannot be traced. NPV - No Par Value Normally the capital of a company is divided into shares representing a 'nominal value' per share such as shares of 1US$ each. No par value shares have no particular nominal value attached to them.

Shark repellant

Often used in risk arbitrage. Examples are golden parachutes, poison pills, safe harbor, and scorched-earth policy. Porcupine provision. Amendment to company charter intended to protect it against takeover.

Shark watcher

Often used in risk arbitrage. Firm specializing in the early detection of takeover activity. Such a firm, whose primary business is usually the solicitation of proxies for client corporations, monitors trading patterns in a client's stock and attempts to determine the identity of parties accumulating shares.

Sharpe benchmark

A statistically created benchmark that adjusts for a manager's index-like tendencies. Named after William Sharpe, Nobel Laureate, and developer of the capital asset pricing model.

Sharpe ratio

A measure of a portfolio's excess return relative to the total variability of the portfolio. Related: Treynor index. Named after William Sharpe, Nobel Laureate, and developer of the capital asset pricing model.

Shelf offering

Offering of registered securities covered by a prospectus whose distribution is not underwritten on a firm commitment basis. The shares may be sold in one block or in small amounts from time to time in agency or principal transactions. See: Rule 415.

Shelf registration

A procedure that allows firms to file one registration statement covering several issues of the same security. SEC Rule 415, adopted in the 1980s, allows a corporation to comply with registration requirements up to two years prior to a public offering of securities. With the registration "on the shelf," the corporation, by simply updating regularly filed annual, quarterly, and related reports to the SEC, can go to the market as conditions become favorable with a minimum of administrative preparation and expense.

Shell corporation

An incorporated company with no significant assets or operations, often formed to obtain financing before beginning actual business, or as a front tax evasion.

Shenzhen Stock Exchange

One of two major securities markets in China.

SHIELD

SHIELD is an interagency export control committee that reviews licenses involving chemical or biological weapons.

Shipment

A shipment is all of the cargo carried under the terms of a single bill of lading.

Shipper's Export Declaration

The SED includes complete particulars on individual shipments and is used to control exports and act as a source document for the official U.S. export statistics. SEDs must be prepared for shipments through the U.S.

Postal Service when the shipment is valued over $500. SEDs are required for shipments, other than by the U.S. Postal Service, where the value of commodities classified under each individual Schedule B number is over $2,500. SEDs must be prepared, regardless of value, for all shipments requiring a validated export license or destined for countries prohibited by the Export Administration Regulations. SEDs are prepared by the exporter and the exporter's agent and delivered to the exporting carrier (such as: post office, airline, or vessel line). The exporting carrier presents the required number of copies to the U.S. Customs Service at the port of export.

The Foreign Trade Statistical Regulations (15 CFR, Part 30) provide the statistical requirements for use by exporters, freight forwarders, and ocean carriers concerning preparation and filing of SEDs.

Shipper's Load and Count

Note on bill of lading indication that the contents of a container were loaded and counted by the shipper and not checked or verified by the Steamship Company.

Shipping Documents

A generic term for the various typesof forms required for overseas shipments, such as commercial invoices, transport documents, packing lists, origin certificates, etc.

Shipping Terms

Terms used in price quotation that include the cost of the merchandise plus the cost of any other services that the beneficiary of a letter of credit had to pay for shipping the merchandise. The "price quote" is embodied in the letter of credit so that the beneficiary will be reimbursed under the letter of credit for the cost of the merchandise plus the cost of the prepaid services.

A. CFR (Cost and Freight) includes:

1.Cost of the merchandise 2.Transportation the dock 3.Loading on vessel 4.Forwarder's fees for preparing the shipping documents. 5.Ocean freight

B. CIF (Cost, Insurance, and Freight) includes:

1.Cost of the merchandise 2.Transportation to dock 3.Loading merchandise on vessel 4.Forwarder's fees for preparing the shipping documents 5.Ocean freight 6.Insurance premium cost

C. CIP (Cost and Insurance) includes:

1.Cost of the merchandise 2.Marine insurance 3.All transportation charges except the ocean freight to the named place of destination.

D. DDP (Exdock Duty Paid) includes:

1.Cost of the merchandise 2.Transportation of merchandise to dock 3.Loading of the merchandise on vessel 4.Forwarder's fee for preparing the shipping documents 5.Ocean Freight 6.Insurance premium cost 7.Unloading of the merchandise at dockside 8.Import duties 9.Delivery to named place of destination.

E. EXW (Ex-Factory) includes cost of the merchandise

FREE ALONGSIDE OR FREE ALONGSIDE STEAMER (FAS) - the seller must deliver the goods to a pier and place them within reach of the ship's loading equipment. The buyer arranges ship space and informs the seller when and where the goods are to be placed.

F. FAS (Free Alongside) includes:

1.Cost of merchandise 2.Transportation to dock 3.Does NOT include forwarder's fees for preparing shipping documentation, such as ocean bills of lading or air way bills.

G. FOB (Free or Freight on Board) includes:

1.Cost of merchandise 2.Transportation to dock 3.Loading on vessel 4.Forwarder's fee for preparing the shipping documents

Shipping Weight

Shipping weight represents the gross weight in kilograms of shipments, including the weight of moisture content, wrappings, crates, boxes, and containers (other than cargo vans and similar substantial outer containers).

Ship's Manifest

An instrument in writing, signed by the captain of a ship, that lists the individual shipments constituting the ship's cargo.

Shirking

The tendency to do less work when the return is smaller. Owners may have more incentive to shirk if they issue equity as opposed to debt, because they retain less ownership interest in the company and therefore may receive a smaller return. Thus, shirking is considered an agency cost of equity.

Shock absorbers

See: Circuit breakers.

Shogun bond

Dollar bond issued in Japan by a nonresident.

Shootout

Venture capital jargon. Refers to two or more venture capital firms fighting for the startup.

Shop

Wall Street slang for a firm.

Shopped stock

Sell inquiry that has been seen by or shown to other dealers before coming to an investment bank.

Shopping

Seeking to obtain the best bid or offer available by calling a number of dealers and/or brokers.

Short

One who has sold a contract to establish a market position and who has not yet closed out this position through an offsetting purchase; the opposite of a long position. Related: Long.

Short against the box

A short sale of a stock is where the seller actually owns the stock, but does not want to close out the position.

Short Bias

In the context of hedge funds, a style of management where part or all of the fund consists of short sales.

Short bonds

Bonds with short (not much time to maturity) current maturities.

Short book

See: Unmatched book.

Short coupon

A bond payment covering less than six-months' interest, because the original issue date is less than six months from the first scheduled interest payment. A bond with a short time to maturity, usually two years or less.

Short covering

Used in the context of general equities. Actual purchase of securities by a short seller to replace those borrowed at the time of a short sale.

Short exempt

Used for listed equity securities. A special trading situation where a short sale is allowed on a minustick. The owners of a convertible trading at parity can sell the equivalent amount of common short on a minus tick, assuming they have the firm intention to convert.

Short hedge

The sale of futures contracts to eliminate or lessen the possible decline in value of an approximately equal amount of the actual financial instrument or physical commodity. Related: Long hedge.

Short interest

Total number of shares of a security that investors have sold short and that have not been repurchased to close out the short position. Usually, investors sell short to profit from price declines. As a result, the short interest is often an indicator of the amount of pessimism in the market about a particular security, although there are other reasons to short that are not related to pessimism. For example, hedging strategies for mergers and acquisition as well as derivative positions may involve short sales.

Short interest theory

The theory that a large interest in short positions in stocks will precede a rise in the market prices, because the short positions must eventually be covered by purchases of the stock.

Short-Form Registration

A procedure that allows a firm to condense its registration statement and prospectus by referencing financial data already on file with the SEC.

Short position

Occurs when a person sells stocks he or she does not yet own. Shares must be borrowed, before the sale, to make "good delivery" to the buyer. Eventually, the shares must be bought back to close out the transaction. This technique is used when an investor believes the stock price will drop.

Short ratio(or short interest ratio)

Number of shares of a security that investors have sold short divided by average daily volume of the security (measured over 30 days or 90 days). There are various interpretations of this ratio. When people short, it is usually (but not always) because they are pessimistic about the security's future performance. Shorting involves buying at at some point however. Hence, some would interpret a high short ratio as an indicator that there will be some buying pressure on the security that would increase its price.

Short-run operating activities

Events and decisions concerning the short-term finance of a firm, such as how much inventory to order and whether to offer cash terms or credit terms to customers.

Short sale

Selling a security that the seller does not own but is committed to repurchasing eventually. It is used to capitalize on an expected decline in the security's price.

Short-sale rule

An SEC rule requiring that short sales be made only in a market that is moving upward; this means either on an uptick from the last sale, or showing no downward movement.

Short selling

Establishing a market position by selling a security one does not own in anticipation of the price of that security falling.

Short settlement

Trade settlement made prior to the standard five-day period due to customer request.

Short-short test

A repealed IRS restriction, that used to limit profits from short-term trading, which three months, to 30% of gross income. The penalty for exceeding this limit would be the loss of certain tax-free benefits.

Short squeeze

When a lack of supply tends to force prices upward. In particular, when prices of a stock or commodity futures contracts start to move up sharply and many traders with short positions are forced to buy stocks or commodities in order to cover their positions and prevent (limit) losses. This sudden surge of buying leads to even higher prices, further aggravating the losses of short sellers who have not covered their positions.

Short straddle

A straddle involves both purchase and sale. In short straddle one put and one call are sold.

Short Supply

Commodities in short supply may be subject to export controls to protect the domestic economy from the excessive drain of scarce materials and to reduce the serious inflationary impact of satisfying foreign demand. Items that the U.S. controls for short supply purposes include petroleum and petroleum products, unprocessed western red cedar, and shipment of horses by sea. The controls are included in the Export Administration Regulations.

Short-term capital gain

A profit on the sale of a security or mutual fund share that has been held for one year or less. A short-term capital gain is taxed as ordinary income.

Short-term interest rates

Interest rates on loan contracts-or debt instruments such as Treasury bills, bank certificates of deposit or commerical paper-having maturities of less than one year. Often called money market rates.

Short-term reserves

Investments in interest-bearing bank deposits, money market instruments, U.S. Treasury bills, and short-term bonds.

Short tender

Practice prohibited by SEC that involves the use of borrowed stock to respond to a tender offer.

Short-term

Any investments with a maturity of one year or less.

Short-term bond fund

A bond mutual fund holding short to intermediate-term bonds that have maturities of three to five years.

Short-term debt

Debt obligations, recorded as current liabilities, requiring payment within the year.

Short-term financial plan

A financial plan that covers the coming fiscal year.

Short-term gain (or loss)

A profit or loss realized from the sale of securities held for less than a year that is taxed at normal income tax rates if the net total is positive.

Short-term investment services

Services that assist firms in making short-term investments.

Short-term solvency ratios

Ratios used to judge the adequacy of liquid assets for meeting short-term obligations as they come due, including (1) the current ratio, (2) the acid test ratio, (3) the inventory turnover ratio, and (4) the accounts receivable turnover ratio.

Short-term tax exempts

Short-term securities issued by states, municipalities, and quesi-government entities such as local housing and urban renewal agencies.

Short-term trend

Erratic price movements that last less than three weeks.

Shortage cost

Costs that fall with increases in the level of investment in current assets.

Shortfall risk

The risk of falling short of any investment target.

Show me buyer/seller

Used in the context of general equities. Customer who has not placed a firm order to buy stock but has requested that the salesperson propose available stock for sale or purchase, along with the asking/bid price. See: Bidding buyer.

Show stopper

A legal barrier, such as a scorched-earth policy or shark repellant system, that firms use to prevent a takeover.

Show and tell list

Used in the context of general equities. Block list which is full of real customer indications (rather than profile).

SHP

The ISO 4217 currency code for the Saint Helena Pound.

Shrinkage

Discrepancy between a firm's actual inventory and its recorded inventory due to theft, deterioration, loss, or clerical problems.

Shut out the book

Used for listed equity securities. Exclude a public bid or offer from participation in a print.

SI

The two-character ISO 3166 country code for SLOVENIA.

SIAC

See: Security Industry Automated Corporation.

SIC

See: Standard Industrial Classification.

Side effects

Effects of a proposed project on other parts of the firm.

Side-by-side trading

Trading a security and an option on the same security on the same exchange.

Sidelines

Hypothetical position referring to noninvolvement in a stock; merely watching.

Sideways market

See: Horizontal price movement.

Sight Draft (S/D)

A draft that is payable upon presentation to the drawee. Compare Date draft and Time draft

Sight Letter of Credit

A letter of credit made payable to a beneficiary upon presentation to the opener of conforming documents.

Signal

To convey information through a firm's actions. The more costly it is to provide a signal, the more credibility it has. For example, to call a press conference and tell everyone that the firm's prospects have improved is less effective than saying the same thing and raising the dividend.

Signaling approach

Notion that insiders in a firm have information that the market does not have, and that the choice of capital structure by insiders can signal information to outsiders and change the value of the firm. This theory is also called the asymmetric information approach.

Signaling approach (on dividend policy)

The argument that dividend changes are important signals to investors about changes in management's expectation about future earnings.

Signature guarantee

The authentication of a signature in the form of a stamp, seal, or written confirmation by a bank or member of a domestic stock exchange (or other acceptable guarantor). A notary public cannot provide a signature guarantee. A signature guarantee is a common requirement when transferring or redeeming shares or changing the ownership of an account.

Signature loan

A good faith loan that is unsecured and requires only the borrower's signature on the loan application.

Signatures on Proxies

The basic rule of acceptability is that if the signature reads as the proxy is printed, it is acceptable. If an individual signs on behalf of another individual and states a legal representation, it is acceptable. Examples: executor, guardian, power of attorney; but not husband, wife, next of kin, etc. On corporate registrations, a manual signature in the name of the Corporation is acceptable. A facsimile signature is also acceptable, but a rubber-stamp signature with a signature line is acceptable only if signed on that line. With joint tenancy, one signature is sufficient, as in the case of one trustee signing for two or more.

Significant influence

The holding of a large portion of the equity of a corporation, usually at least 20%, which gives the holder a significant amount of control over the corporation. This degree of holding must be recorded in a firm's financial statements.

Significant order

An order to buy or sell a large enough quantity of securities that the price of the security may be affected. Institutional investors usually spread out such an order over a few days or weeks to avoid adverse pressures on the buy or sell price.

Significant order imbalance

A large number of buy or sell orders for a stock that cause an abnormally wide spread between bid and offer prices, and often causes the exchange to halt the sale of the stock until significant balance has been reestablished.

Silent partner

A partner in a business who has no role in management but shares in the liability, tax responsibility, and cash flow.

Silver Parachutes

These provisions are similar to Golden Parachutes in that they provide severance payments upon a change in corporate control, but unlike Golden Parachutes, a large number of a firm's employees are eligible for these benefits.

SIMEX

See: Singapore International Monetary Exchange.

Simple compound growth method

Calculating a growth rate by relating terminal value to initial value and assuming a constant percentage annual rate of growth between the two values.

Simple interest

Interest calculated as a simple percentage of the original principal amount. Compare to compound interest.

Simple IRA

A salary deduction plan for retirement benefits provided by some small companies with no more than 100 employees.

Simple linear regression

A regression analysis between only two variables, one dependent and the other explanatory.

Simple linear trend model

An extrapolative statistical model that asserts that earnings have a base level and grow at a constant amount each period.

Simple moving average

The mean, calculated at any time over a past period of fixed length.

Simple prospect

An investment opportunity in which only two outcomes are possible.

Simple rate of return

The return from investments figured by dividing income plus capital gains by the amount of capital invested. The effect of compounding is not taken into account.

Simplified Employee Pension (SEP) plan

A pension plan in which both the employee and the employer contribute to an individual retirement account. Also available to the self-employed.

Simulation

The use of a mathematical model to imitate a situation many times in order to estimate the likelihood of various possible outcomes. See: Monte Carlo simulation.

Singapore-Jahor-Riau Growth Triangle

SIJORI is a subregional economic grouping composed of the nation of Singapore, the Malaysian State of Johor, and Indonesia's Riau Province.

Singapore International Monetary Exchange (SIMEX)

A leading futures and options exchange in Singapore.

Single-buyer policy

Ex-Im Bank practice allows the exporter to insure certain transactions selectively.

Single-country fund

A mutual fund that invests in individual countries outside the United States.

Single Currency Peg

See: Exchange Rate Classifications.

Single European Act

The SEA, which entered into force in July 1987, was the first significant revision of the Treaty of Rome. The SEA provides the legal and procedural support for achievement of the single European Market by 1992. The SEA revised the EEC Treaty and, where not already provided for in the Treaty, majority decisions were introduced for numerous votes facing the Council of Ministers, particularly those affecting establishment of the single European Market and the European financial common market. The role of the European Parliament was strengthened; decisions on fiscal matters remained subject to unanimity.

Single-factor model

A model of security returns that acknowledges only one common factor. The single factor is usually the market return. See: Factor model.

Single-index model

A model of stock returns that decomposes influences on returns into a systematic factor, as measured by the return on the broad market index, and firm specific factors. Related: Market Model

Single Internal Market Information Service

SIMIS, operated by the Commerce Department's International Trade Administration, provides information, assistance, and advice on how to do business in the European Community's internal market. Telephone: 202-482-5276.

Single life annuity

An annuity covering one person. A straight life annuity provides payments until death, while a life annuity with a guaranteed period provides payments until death or continues payments to a beneficiary for a guaranteed term, such as ten years.

Single option

A single put option or call option, as opposed to a spread or straddle, which involves multiple puts and calls.

Single-payment bond

A bond that makes only one payment of principal and interest.

Single-Premium Deferred Annuity (SPDA)

An IRA-like annuity into which an investor makes a lump-sum payment that is invested in either a fixed-return instrument or a variable-return portfolio, which is taxed only when distributions are taken.

Single-premium life insurance

A whole life insurance policy requiring one premium payment, which accrues cash value much more quickly than a policy paid in installments.

Single-state municipal bond fund

A mutual fund investing only in government obligations within a single state, with state tax-free dividends, but taxed capital gains.

Sinker

A bond with interest and principal payments coming from the proceeds of a sinking fund.

Sinking fund

A fund to which money is added on a regular basis that is used to ensure investor confidence that promised payments will be made and that is used to redeem debt securities or preferred stock issues.

Sinking fund requirement

A condition included in some corporate bond indentures that requires the issuer to retire a specified portion of debt each year. Any principal due at maturity is called the balloon maturity.

Sistema de Informacion al Comercio Exterior

SICE (English: Foreign Trade Information System) is a databank which provides foreign trade information to the public and private sectors of member countries of the Organization of American States (OAS). The System includes information on the U.S. import and export markets, markets of other OAS member countries, and trade information on the European Community and Japan.

Sistema Economico Latinoamericano

See: Latin American Economic System.

SIT

The ISO 4217 currency code for the Slovenian Tolar.

Sit tight

Directive from the trader to the customer to be patient, emphasizing that one's piece of business will be executed.

Size

Refers to the magnitude of an offering, an order, or a trade. Large as in the size of an offering, the size of an order, or the size of a trade. Size is relative from market to market and security to security. "I can buy size at 102-22," means that a trader can buy a significant amount at 102-22. Small is <10,000 shares. Medium is 15,000-25,000 shares. Good is 50,000 shares. Size is 100,000 shares. Good six-figure size is 200,000-300,000 shares. Multiple six-figure size is >300,000 shares. Size of the market is actual number of shares represented in one's market, or bid and offering; unless specified, assumed to be at least 500 to 1000 shares, depending on the stock.

Size out the book

Overt action to exclude a public bid or offer from participation in a print through trading a larger size in the book. Can never size out a market order. See: Priority, shut out the book.

SJ

The two-character ISO 3166 country code for SVALBARD AND JAN MAYEN.

SK

The two-character ISO 3166 country code for SLOVAKIA.

Skewed distribution

Probability distribution in which an unequal number of observations lie below (negative skew) or above (positive skew) the mean.

Skewness

Negative skewness means there is a substantial probability of a big negative return. Positive skewness means that there is a greater-than-normal probability of a big positive return.

Skill

The ability to accurately forecast returns. We measure skill using the information coefficient.

Skip-day settlement

Settling a trade one business day beyond what is normal.

Skip-payment privilege

A mortgage contract clause giving borrowers the right to skip payments if they are ahead of schedule.

SKK

The ISO 4217 currency code for the Slovak Republic Koruna.

Skort-Swing Transaction

Any purchase and sale, or sale and purchase, of the issuer's equity securities by an insider within a period of less than six months, See: Section 16(b) above.

SL

The two-character ISO 3166 country code for SIERRA LEONE.

SLD last sale

Shortened version of "sold last sale," which shows up on the consolidated tape when a large change (one point for lower priced securities and two points for higher-priced securities) occurs between transactions.

Sleeper

Stock in which there is little investor interest but that has significant potential to gain in price once its attractions are recognized. Antithesis of high flyer.

Sleeping beauty

Often used in risk arbitrage. Potential takeover target that has not yet been approached by an acquirer. Such a company usually has particularly attractive features, such as a large amount of cash, or undervalued real estate or other assets.

Slippage

The difference between estimated transactions costs and actual transactions costs. The difference usually represents revisions to price difference or spread and commission costs.

SLL

The ISO 4217 currency code for the Sierra Leone Leone.

Slump

A temporary fall in performance, often describing consistently falling security prices for several weeks or months.

SM

The two-character ISO 3166 country code for SAN MARINO.

Small business policy

Insurance coverage available to new exporters and small businesses.

Small-cap

A stock with a small capitalization, meaning a total equity value of less than $500 million.

Small-capitalization (small-cap) fund

A mutual fund that invests primarily in stocks of companies whose market value is less than $1 billion. Small-cap stocks historically have been more volatile than large-cap stocks, and often perform differently from the overall market.

Small-capitalization (small cap) stocks

The stocks of companies whose market value is less than $1 billion. Small-cap companies tend to grow faster than large-cap companies and typically use any profits for expansion rather to pay dividends. They also are more volatile than large-cap companies, and have a higher failure rate.

Small-firm effect

The tendency of small firms (in terms of total market capitalization) to outperform the stock market (consisting of both large and small firms).

Small investor

An individual person investing in small quantities of stock or bonds. This group of investors makes up a minimal fraction of total stock ownership.

Small issues exemption

Securities issues that involve less than $1.5 million are not required to file a registration statement with the SEC. Instead, they are governed by Regulation A, for which only a brief offering statement is needed.

Small Order Execution System (SOES)

Three-tiered system of automatic execution of an order at the best price. Size is either 200, 500, or, most often, 1000 shares.

Smart money

Investors who make consistent profits in the market, regardless of the investing environment, by making wise, educated moves.

SMBS

See: Stripped mortgage backed securities.

Smidge

Small amount of price, usually +/- 1/8 or 1/4.

Smithsonian Agreement

A revision to the Bretton Woods international monetary system that was signed at the Smithsonian Institution in Washington, D.C., in December 1971. Included were a new set of par values, widened bands to +/- 2.25% of par, and an increase in the official value of gold to US$38.00 per ounce.

SN

The two-character ISO 3166 country code for SENEGAL.

Snake

Arrangement established in 1972, that ties European currencies to each other within specified limits.

Snowballing

Used in the context of general equities. Process by which the exercise of stop orders in a declining or advancing market causes further downward or upward pressure on prices, thus triggering more stop orders and more price pressure, and so on.

SO

The two-character ISO 3166 country code for SOMALIA.

Social Security benefits

Monthly government payments to retired workers or their families who have paid Social Security taxes for a total of 40 quarters or 10 years.

Social Security Disability Income Insurance

Program financed by the Social Security tax to provide assistance to disabled individuals with disabilities expected to last at least one year, to compensate for lost income.

Socially conscious mutual fund

A mutual fund that does not invest in companies that have interests in socially unacceptable markets or produce harmful products or by-products, such as high levels of environmental pollution.

Sociedad Anonima - S.A.

Spanish meaning "incorporated company": is a form of corporation which must have at least five shareholders, who may be either Mexican or foreign. Each shareholder is liable only up to the amount of their contribution. No shares may be held by the company name. "S.A." must follow the firm name, indicating that it is a corporation.

Sociedad Anonima de Capital Variable - SA de CV

Spanish meaning "variable capital company": similarly to SA, must have at least five shareholders, who may be either Mexican or foreign. Each shareholder is liable only up to the amount of their contribution. SA de CV differs from SA in that an SA de CV may own its shares. "S.A. de C.V." must follow the firm name indicating that it a corporation with variable capital.

Societate a Responsabilitate Limitata - "Srl"

Italian private company.

Societate in Nome Collettivo - "Snc"

Italian general partnership in which there is no limit on the liability of the partners.

Societate Per Azioni - "SpA"

Italian public corporation: must have at least two shareholders at formation; after formation, the requirement is reduced to one shareholder.

Société Anonyme - S.A.

French: meaning "incorporated" - is a form of corporation which must have at least seven shareholders, who may be either French or foreign. Each member is liable only up to the amount of stock owned.

Société à Responsabilité Limitée – SARL

French meaning "limited liability company": has features of both a corporation and a partnership. The number of partners cannot exceed 50. Partners may be either French or foreign. Partner liabilities are limited to the amount of their contribution, which may be in cash or in kind but not in skills. While shares may be freely traded among partners, they may not be transferred to third parties without majority agreement of partners represenating at least 75 percent of the capital.

Société en Commandité Simple

French meaning "limited partnership": is composed of general partners, of which the managing partner at least must have unlimited liability, and silent partners whose liability is limited to the amount of their capital contributions. Silent partners are not permitted to perform any management functions vis-a-vis other partners. In a limited partnership without shares, transfer of shares of the limited partners is only allowable with the consent of all the partners. In a limited partnership with shares (Soci,t, en commandit, par actions), these are transferred in a manner similar to corporations.

Société en Nom Collectif – SNC

French meaning "general partnership": is organized with all partners being allocated shares for their contributions, which may be cash, in-kind, or services. There is no required minimum or maximum capital, nor any share par value. Shares in the firm are not negotiable and cannot be transferred without agreement of all the partners. Each partner is liable for the totality of the firm's debts and obligations.

Société Internationale Financière pour les Investissements et le Développement en Afrique – SIFIDA

SIFIDA fosters the formation of profitable business in Africa by identifying and nurturing productive projects, by arranging for syndicated loans, and by providing export finance. The Society is a holding company affiliated with the African Development Bank (AfDB); headquarters are in Chêne-Bourg, Switzerland. Major shareholders include the AfDB, the International Finance Corporation and more than 100 financial, industrial, and commercial institutions around the world.

Société par Actions Simplifiée – SAS

French meaning "private limited company": is designed for joint ventures and permits the rights and liability of each shareholder to be defined by mutual agreement between the parties. Only two shareholders are required.

Society for Worldwide Interbank Financial Telecommunications

SWIFT is a cooperative organized under Belgian law, with headquarters in La Hulpe, near Brussels. SWIFT provides communications services to the international banking industry, including payments and administrative messages and, more recently, securities settlements. Traffic in 1991 was about 362 million messages. SWIFT is owned by the member banks — approximately 1,600 — including the central banks of most countries. The U.S. Federal Reserve is not a member, but participates in certain types of payments. Securities brokers and dealers, clearing and depository institutions, exchanges for securities, and travelers checks issuers also participate in SWIFT. SWIFT was organized in 1973 and started operations in 1977.

SOES

See: Small Order Execution System.

"Soft" capital rationing

Constraints on spending that under certain circumstances can be violated or even viewed as constituting targets rather than absolute limits.

Soft Currency

The currency of a nation in which exchange may be made only with difficulty. Soft currency countries typically have minimal exchange reserves and deficits in their balance of payments. See: Hard Currency.

Soft dollars

The value of research services that brokerage houses supply to investment managers "free of charge" in exchange for the investment manager's business commissions.

Soft landing

A term describing a growth rate high enough to keep the economy out of recession, but also slow enough to prevent high inflation and interest rates.

Soft Loan

Commonly, a loan from a government or multilateral development bank with a long repayment period and below-market interest.

Soft market

A buyer's market in which supply exceeds demand, causing little trading activity and wide bid-ask spreads.

Soft spot

Stocks or groups of stocks that remain weak in a strong market.

Softs

Tropical commodities such as coffee, sugar, and cocoa.

Sold away

Refers to over-the-counter trading. Having sold stock to another dealer before making the present offering.

Sold-out market

Unavailability of a futures contract in a particular commodity or maturity date because of contract executions and limited offerings.

Sole proprietorship

A business owned by a single individual. A sole proprietor pays no corporate income tax but has unlimited liability for business debts and obligations.

Solvency

Ability to meet obligations.

SOS

The ISO 4217 currency code for the Somalian Shilling.

Sour bond

A bond issue that has defaulted on interest or principal payments, and will thus trade at a large discount and a poor credit rating.

Source of funds seller

Customer seller of stock for the purpose of raising cash for other purchases. Such a seller will sell only at advantageous prices, and not aggressively.

Sources and applications of funds statement

See: Statement of cash flows

South African Futures Exchange (SAFEX)

Electronic futures and options exchange based in South Africa.

South Asian Association for Regional Cooperation

SAARC promotes economic, technical, scientific, and social cooperation among members. The Association was founded in 1985 by seven countries: Bangladesh, Bhutan, India, Maldives, Nepal, Pakistan, and Sri Lanka. The Association plans to establish a South Asian Preferential Trading Arrangement (SAPTA) by 1997 as a step toward creating an economic community in south Asia.

Southern Africa Development Community

SADC, established in April 1980 (as the Southern Africa Development Coordination Conference), is a regional economic pact comprising Angola, Botswana, Lesotho, Malawi, Mozambique, Namibia, Swaziland, Tanzania, Zambia, and Zimbabwe. Since a change in name and focus in mid-1992, the Community focuses solely on development, leaving trade matters to the Preferential Trade Agreement for Eastern and Southren Africa (PTA). Community headquarters are in Gaborone, Botswana.

Southern African Customs Union

SACU, established in 1910, includes Botswana, Lesotho, Namibia, South Africa, and Swaziland. SACU provides for the free exchange of goods within the area, a common external tariff, and a sharing of custom revenues. External tariffs, excise duties, and several rebate and refund provisions are the same for all SACU members. SACU's revenues are apportioned among its members according to a set formula. These funds constitute a significant contribution to each member's government revenues.

Southern Cone

The southern cone consists of Argentina, Brazil, Chile, Paraguay, and Uruguay. With the exception of Chile, these countries also comprise the Southern Common Market.

South Pacific Forum

The SPF is a regional arrangement for convening 15 governments and territories for deliberations on issues of mutual interest. The Forum was established in 1971; headquarters are in Suva, Fiji; members include: Australia, the Cook Islands, Fiji, Kirbati, Marshall Islands, Micronesia, Nauru, New Zealand, Niue, Papua New Guinea, Samoa, Solomon Island, Tonga, Tuvalu, and Vanatu. The South Pacific Bureau for Economic Cooperation (SPEC) is a subsidiary organization which promotes regional cooperation in the development of the island members in partnership with the more industrially developed countries of the region: Australia and New Zealand.

Sovereign risk

The risk that a central bank will impose foreign exchange regulations that will reduce or negate the value of FX contracts. Also refers to the risk of government default on a loan made to a country or guaranteed by it.

SOXS

See: Sarbanes Oxley Act of 2002.

S&P

Standard & Poor's Corporation.

S&P 500 Composite Index

Index of 500 widely held common stocks that measures the general performance of the market.

S&P phenomenon

Tendency of stocks newly added to the S&P composite index to rise in price due to a large number of buy orders as S&P-related index funds add the stock to their portfolios.

S&P Rating

Rating service provided by S&P that indicates the amount of risk involved with different securities.

Span

To cover all contingencies within a specified range.

SPDRs

SPDRs (Spiders) are designed to track the value of the Standard & Poor's 500 Composite Price Index. Stands for Standard & Poor's Depositary Receipt. They trade on the American Stock Exchange under the symbol SPY. SPDRs are similar to closed-end funds but are formally known as, a unit investment trust. One SPDR unit is valued at approximately one-tenth (1/10) of the value of the S&P 500. Dividends are disbursed quarterly, and are based on the accumulated stock dividends held in trust, less any expenses of the trust. See: Mid-cap SPDR.

Special American Business Internship Training Program

SABIT, originally the Soviet-American Business Internship Training Program, is a cooperative program that brings business executives and scientists from the former Soviet Union for three-to six-month internships with American companies. The program teaches these managers and scientists how to operate in a market economy at the same time that American businesses development market contacts once their interns return home. Soviet business managers are referred by the Commerce Department's International Trade Administration to sponsoring U.S. companies, which make the final selection of their interns. The program matches U.S. corporate sponsors with Soviet business executives from the same industries. The Independent States provide transportation; the companies provide living expenses and training in management techniques (production, distribution, marketing, accounting, wholesaling, and publishing).

Special and Differential Treatment

The principle, enunciated in the Tokyo Declaration, that the Tokyo Round negotiations should seek to accord particular benefits to the exports of developing countries, consistent with their trade, financial, and development needs. Among proposals for special or differential treatment are reduction or elimination of tariffs applied to exports of developing countries under the Generalized System of Preferences (GSP), expansion of product and country coverage of the GSP, accelerated implementation of tariff cuts agreed to in the Tokyo Round for developing country exports, substantial reduction or elimination of tariff escalation, special provisions for developing country exports in any new codes of conduct covering nontariff measures, assurance that any new multilateral safeguard system will contain special provisions for developing country exports, and the principle that developed countries will expect less than full reciprocity for trade concessions they grant developing countries.

Special arbitrage account

A margin account with lower cash requirements, reserved for transactions that are hedged by an offsetting position in futures or options.

Special assessment bond

A municipal bond with interest paid by the taxes of the community benefiting from the bond-funded project.

Special bid

A method of purchasing a large block of stock on the NYSE by advertising a client's large buy order, and matching it up with a number of other traders' smaller sell orders.

Special bond account

A special broker margin account used only for transactions in US government bonds, municipals, and eligible listed and unlisted non-convertible corporate bonds.

Special dividend

Also referred to as an extra dividend. Dividend that is unlikely to be repeated.

Special Drawing Rights

SDRs are international reserve assets, created by the International Monetary Fund (IMF) in 1970 and allocated to individual member nations. Within conditions set by the IMF, SDRs can be used by a nation with a deficit in its balance of international payments to settle debts with another nation or with the IMF. The value of SDRs is computed as a weighted average of five currencies: deutsche mark, French franc, Japanese yen, pound sterling, and U.S. dollar.

Specially Designated Nationals

The Office of Foreign Assets Control (OFAC), Department of the Treasury, implements and enforces financial and trade sanctions. FAC has the authority to include within the definition of the sanctioned government those individuals and entities that FAC has determined are owned by, controlled by, or acting directly or indirectly on behalf of the target government. Parties so identified are known as Specially Designated Nationals or SDNs. In practice, an SDN is a target government body, representative, intermediary, or front (whether overt or covert) that usually is located in a third country and functions as an extension of the sanctioned government. An SDN may also be a third-party company that otherwise becomes owned or controlled by the target government or that operates on its behalf. No criminal linkage is necessary. Ownership by, control by, acting on behalf of, or profiting from trade with the target government or country would suffice to qualify a person for designation.

Specialist

On an exchange, the member firm that is designated as the market maker (or dealer for a listed common stock). Member of a stock exchange who maintains a "fair and orderly market" in one or more securities. Only one specialist can be designated for a given stock, but dealers may be specialists for several stocks. In contrast, there can be multiple market makers in the OTC market. Major functions include executing limit orders on behalf of other exchange members for a portion of the floor broker's commission, and buying or selling for the specialist's own account to counteract temporary imbalances in supply and demand and thus prevent wide swings in stock prices.

Specialist block purchase and sale

Purchase of a large number of securities by a specialist for himself or to pass on to another floor trader or block buyer.

Specialist market

Market in a stock made solely by the specialist, as no public orders, and henceforth no depth, exist in the market.

Specialist unit

A specialist who maintains a stable market by acting as a principal and agent for other brokers in one or many stocks.

Specialist's book

Chronological record maintained by a specialist that includes the specialist's own inventory of securities, market orders to sell short, and limit orders and stop orders that other stock exchange members have placed with the specialist.

Specialist's short-sale ratio

The percentage of the total short sales of stock sold short by specialists.

Special Meeting

Refers to a meeting of shareholders outside the usual annual general meeting. In the context of corporate governance, some limitations either increase the level of shareholder support required to call a special meeting beyond that specified by state law or eliminate the ability to call one entirely. Such provisions add an extra time delay to many proxy fights, since bidders must wait until the regularly scheduled annual meeting to replace board members or dismantle takeover defenses.

Special Policy of Insurance

Document issued on behalf of the Underwriter stating the terms and conditions of the marine insurance. Issued when evidence of insurance is required, as by the bank issuing the Letter of Credit.

Special-Purpose Entity

A financing technique in which a company decreases its risk by creating separate partnerships, rather than subsidiaries, for certain holdings and solicits outside investors to take on the risk. In order to qualify as a special-purpose entity, whose financial results are not carried on the company's books, the unit must meet strict accounting guidelines. Compare to subsidary.

Special 301

The Special 301 statute requires the United States Trade Representative (USTR) to review annually the condition of intellectual property protection among U.S. trading partners. Submissions are accepted from industry after which the USTR, weighing all relevant information, makes a determination as to whether a country presents excessive barriers to trade with the United States by virtue of its inadequate protection of intellectual property. If the USTR makes a positive determination, a country may be named to the list of: (a) Priority Foreign Countries (the most egregious), (b) the Priority Watch List, or (c) the Watch List. Special 301 (a variation of Section 301) was created by the Omnibus Trade and Competitiveness Act of 1988. See: Section 301, Super 301.

Specification

A clear and complete descriptive statement covering the technical point of any item ordered. A specification using a proprietary name or equal is acceptable.

Specific issues market

The market in which dealers reverse in securities they wish to short.

Specific Return

The part of the excess return not explained by common factors. The specific return is independent of (uncorrelated with) the common factors and the specific returns to other assets. It is also called the idiosyncratic return.

Specific risk

See: Unique risk.

Spectail

A dealer doing business with retail but concentrating more on acquiring and financing its own speculative positions.

Speculation

Purchasing risky investments that present the possibility of large profits, but also pose a higher-than-average possibility of loss. A profitable strategy over the long term if undertaken by professionals who hedge their portfolios to control the amount of risk.

Speculative

Securities that involve a high level of risk.

Speculative demand (for money)

The need for cash to take advantage of investment opportunities that may arise.

Speculative-grade bond

Bond rated Ba or lower by Moody's, or BB or lower by S&P, or an unrated bond.

Speculative motive

A desire to hold cash in order to be poised to exploit any attractive investment opportunity requiring a cash expenditure that might arise.

Speculative stock

Very risky stock.

Speculator

One who attempts to anticipate price changes and, through buying and selling contracts, aims to make profits. A speculator does not use the market in connection with the production, processing, marketing, or handling of a product. See: Trader.

Speed

Related: Prepayment speed.

Spider

See: SPDRs.

Spike

Order ticket that shows the stock, price, number of shares, type, and account of the order. Origin: Practice of placing the ticket on a metal spike upon execution or cancellation.) Spike is also a sudden, drastic increase in a company's share price.

Spin-off

A company can create an independent company from an existing part of the company by selling or distributing new shares in the so-called spin-off.

Spinning

In investment banking, the practice of an investment bank setting aside portions of a corporation's Initial Public Offering for senior management of that corporation. Ethically questionable practice which appears to be a form of bribery.

SPINs

Stands for Standard & Poor's 500 Index Subordinated Notes.

Split

Sometimes, companies split their outstanding shares into more shares. If a company with 1 million shares executes a two-for-one split, the company would have 2 million shares. An investor with 100 shares before the split would hold 200 shares after the split. The investor's percentage of equity in the company remains the same, and the share price of the stock owned is one-half the price of the stock on the day prior to the split.

Split commission

A commission shared between a broker and a financial adviser or other professional who brought the customer to the broker.

Split-coupon bond

A bond that begins as a zero-coupon bond paying no interest and converts to an interest paying bond on a future date.

Split-fee option

An option on an option. The buyer generally executes the split fee with first an initial fee, with a window period at the end of which (upon payment of a second fee) the original terms of the option may be extended to a later predetermined final notification date.

Split offering

A municipal bond issue that is made up of serial bonds and term maturity bonds.

Split order

A large securities transaction that is divided into smaller orders that are spread out over some period of time to avoid large fluctuations in the market price.

Split print

Block trade printed at two different prices. Often used in dividend rolls to get an average price equal to the dividend.

Split-rate tax system

A tax system that taxes retained earnings at a higher rate than earnings that are distributed as dividends.

Split rating

Two different ratings given to the same security by two important rating agencies.

Split stock

(1) Purchases or sales shared with others. (2) Division of the outstanding shares of a corporation into a large number of shares. Ordinarily, splits must be proposed by directors and approved by shareholders.

Spoken for

Amount of opposite demand (placement) or supply (availability) the trader has in efforts to cross the stock. Not open.

Sponsor

An underwriting investment company that offers shares in its mutual funds, or an influential institution that highly values a particular security and thus creates additional demand for the security.

Spontaneous Current Liabilities

Short-term obligations that automatically increase and decrease in response to financing needs, such as accounts payable.

Spontaneous Liabilities

Obligations that arise automatically in the course of operating a business when a firm buys goods and services on credit.

Spot commodity

A commodity that is traded with the expectation of actual delivery, as opposed to a commodity future that is usually not delivered.

Spot Exchange

The purchase or sale of foreign exchange for immediate delivery.

Spot exchange rates

Exchange rate on currency for immediate delivery. Related: Forward exchange rate.

Spot futures parity theorem

Describes the theoretically correct relationship between spot and futures prices. Violation of the parity relationship gives rise to arbitrage opportunities.

Spot interest rate

Interest rate fixed today on a loan that is made today. Related: Forward interest rates.

Spot lending

Originating mortgages by processing applications taken directly from prospective borrowers.

Spot markets

Related: Cash markets.

Spot month

The nearest delivery month on a futures contract.

Spot price

The current market price of the actual physical commodity. Also called cash price. Current delivery price of a commodity traded in the spot market, in which goods are sold for cash and delivered immediately. Antithesis of futures price.

Spot rate

The theoretical yield on a zero-coupon Treasury security.

Spot rate curve

The graphical depiction of the relationship between the spot rates and maturity.

Spot secondary

Secondary distribution that may not require an SEC registration statement and may be attempted without delay. An underwriting discount is normally included in these offerings.

Spot trade

The purchase and sale of a foreign currency, commodity, or other item for immediate delivery.

Spot transaction

A foregin exchange transaction in which each party promises to pay a certain amount of currency to the other on the same day or within one or two days.

Spousal IRA

An individual retirement account in the name of an unemployed spouse.

Spousal remainder trust

A fixed-term trust from which income is distributed to the beneficiary (such as a child of the grantor) to take advantage of a lower tax bracket, and that at the end of the term passes to the grantor's spouse.

Spread

(1) The gap between bid and ask prices of a stock or other security. (2) The simultaneous purchase and sale of separate futures or options contracts for the same commodity for delivery in different months. Also known as a straddle. (3) Difference between the price at which an underwriter buys an issue from a firm and the price at which the underwriter sells it to the public. (4) The price an issuer pays above a benchmark fixed-income yield to borrow money.

Spread income

Also called margin income, the difference between income and cost. For a depository institution, the difference between the assets it invests in (loans and securities) and the cost of its funds (deposits and other sources).

Spread option

A position consisting of the purchase of one option and the sale of another option on the same underlying security with a different exercise price and/or expiration date.

Spread order

An order listing the series of options that the customer wants to buy and sell and the desired spread between the premiums paid and received for the options.

Spread position

The status of an account after a spread order has been carried out.

Spread strategy

A strategy that involves a position in one or more options so that the cost of buying an option is funded entirely or in part by selling another option in the same underlying. Also called spreading.

Spreadsheet

A computer program that organizes numerical data into rows and columns in order to calculate and make adjustments based on new data.

Sprinkling trust

A trust in which the trustee decides how to distribute trust income among a group of designated people.

SPX

Applies to derivative products. Symbol for the S&P 500 index.

Squeeze

Period when stocks or commodities futures increase in price and investors who have sold short must cover their short positions to prevent loss of large amounts of money.

SR

The two-character ISO 3166 country code for SURINAME.

SRG

The ISO 4217 currency code for the Surinam Guilder.

SS1

Securities sales speaker box that transmits to all investment banks' regional trading and sales desks.

ST

The two-character ISO 3166 country code for SAO TOME AND PRINCIPE.

Stabilization

The action undertakes a country when it buys and sells its own currency to protect its exchange value. Actions registered competitive traders undertake by on the

NYSE to meet the exchange requirement that 75% of their traded be stabilizing, meaning that sell orders follow a plus tick and buy orders a minus tick. Actions a managing underwriter undertake so that the market price does not fall below the public offering price during the offering period.

Stable Paretian, or Fractal Hypothesis

In the characteristic function of the fractal family of distributions, the characteristic exponent alpha can range between one and two. See: Alpha, Fractal Distributions, Gaussian.

Stability

The relative steadiness or safety of a security or fund compared to the market as a whole. For example, money market funds and other short-term investments offer more stability than funds that invest in growth stocks.

Stag

Speculator who buys and sells stocks to hold for short intervals to make quick profits.

Stagflation

A period of slow economic growth and high unemployment with rising prices (inflation).

Staggered board of directors

Occurs when a portion of directors are elected periodically, instead of all at once. Board terms are often staggered in order to thwart unfriendly takeover attempts, since potential acquirers would have to wait longer before they could take control of a company's board through the normal voting procedure.

Staggering maturities

Hedging against interest rate movements by investment in short-, medium-, and long-term bonds.

Stagnation

A period of slow economic growth, or, in securities trading, a period of inactive trading.

Stakeholders

All parties that have an interest, financial or otherwise, in a firm-stockholders, creditors, bondholders, employees, customers, management, the community, and the government.

Stalking horse

In bankruptcy proceedings, this refers to the company that first bids for the companies assets.

Stalking horse bid

In bankruptcy proceedings, this refers to first bid for the companies assets. This is the bid to beat. If there are multiple bids, often there is a bankruptcy auction.

Stamp duty

Applies mainly to international equities. Taxes on foreign transactions, usually a percentage of total transaction amount, that can be unilateral or bilateral in nature.

Stamp tax

Tax on a financial transaction.

Stand-alone principle

Investment approach that advocates a firm should accept or reject a project by comparing it with securities in the same risk class.

Standard deduction

The IRS-specified amount by which a taxpayer is entitled to reduce income an alternative to itemizing deductions.

Standard deviation

The square root of the variance. A measure of dispersion of a set of data from its mean.

Standard error

In statistics, a measure of the possible error in an estimate. Plus or minus 2 standard errors usually provides a 95% confidence interval.

Standard Industrial Classification (SIC) system

The system established by the U.S. government for defining industries and classifying individual establishments by industry.

Standard International Trade Classification

The SITC was developed by the United Nations in 1950 and is used solely by international organizations for reporting international trade. The SITC has been revised several times; the current version is Revision 3.

Standardized normal distribution

A normal distribution with a mean of 0 and a standard deviation of 1.

Standardized value

Also called the normal deviate, the distance of one data point from the mean, divided by the standard deviation of the distribution.

Standard & Poor's MidCap 400 Index

A market capitalization-weighted benchmark index made up of 400 securities with market values between $200 million and $5 billion.

Standard & Poor's SmallCap 600 Index

A small-capitalization benchmark index made up of 600 domestic stocks chosen for market size, liquidity, and industry group representation.

Standards

As defined by the Multilateral Trade Negotiations "Agreement on Technical Barriers to Trade" (Standards Code), a standard is a technical specification contained in a document that lays down characteristics of a product such as levels of quality, performance, safety, or dimensions. Standards may include, or deal exclusively with, terminology, symbols, testing and test methods, packaging, marking, or labeling requirements as they apply to a product.

The GATT Standards Code, negotiated and accepted during the Tokyo Round in the 1970s, is designed to eliminate the use of standards, technical regulations, and conformity assessment (certification) procedures as unnecessary barriers to trade. The Standards Code is administered by the GATT Secretariat in Geneva, Switzerland. The Commerce Department's National Institute of Standards and Technology is responsible for several provisions of the Standards Code which relate to the establishment of a U.S. inquiry point, a standards information center, and a technical office for non-agricultural products.

Stand-By Arrangements

A stand-by arrangement, like an extended arrangement, assures a member country of the International Monetary Fund (IMF) that it will be able to make purchases up to a specified amount from the IMF during a given period, as long as the member has observed the performance criteria and other terms specified in the arrangement. Stand-by arrangements extend up to three years. See: International Monetary Fund.

Standby commitment

An agreement between a corporation and investment firm that the firm will purchase whatever part of a stock issue that is offered in a rights offering that is not subscribed to in the two- to four- week standby period.

Standby fee

Amount paid to an underwriter who agrees to purchase any stock that is not purchased by public investors in a rights offering.

Standby letter of credit

Agreement to guarantee invoice payments to a supplier; a standby LOC promises to pay the seller if the buyer fails to pay.

Standing

Level of priority in the trading crowd.

Standstill

Standstill refers to a commitment of GATT contracting parties not to impose new trade-restrictive measures during the Uruguay Round negotiations. See: Rollback.

Standstill agreement

Contract by which the bidding firm in a takeover attempt agrees to limit its holdings of another firm.

Stand up to

Make a good-sized market in the trader's own bid and offering prices. Hence, "standing up" to the bid signifies the trader's willingness to buy size (i.e., 50m) volume at the advertised bid, even if the customer buyer/ seller falls down.

Start-up

The earliest stage of a new business venture.

State bank

A bank authorized in a specific state by a state-based charter, with generally the same functions as a national bank.

State and local government series (SLUGs)

Special nonmarketable certificates, notes, and bonds offered to state and local governments as a means to invest proceeds from their own tax-exempt financing. Interest rates and maturities comply with IRS arbitrage provisions. Slugs are offered in both time deposit and demand deposit forms. Time deposit certificates have maturities of up to one year. Notes mature in one to ten years and bonds mature in more than ten years. Demand deposit securities are one-day certificates rolled over with a rate adjustment daily.

Stated annual interest rate

The interest rate expressed as a per year percentage, by which interest payments are determined. See: Annual percentage rate.

Stated conversion price

At the time of issuance of a convertible security, the price the issuer effectively grants the securityholder to purchase the common stock, equal to the par value of the convertible security divided by the conversion ratio.

Stated maturity

For the CMO tranche, the date the last payment would occur at zero CPR.

Stated value

A monetary worth figure that bears no relation to market value that is assigned, for accounting purposes, to stock for use instead of par value.

State Export Program Database

The SEPD is a trade lead system maintained by the National Association of State Development Agencies (NASDA). The SEPD includes information on state operated trade lead systems.

Statement of Additional Information (SAI)

A document provided as a supplement to a mutual fund prospectus. It provides more detailed information about fund policies, operations, and risks. Also known as a Part B prospectus.

Statement billing

Billing method in which the sales for a period such as a month (for which a customer also receives invoices) are collected into a single statement, and the customer must pay all the invoices represented on the statement.

Statement of Cash Flows

A financial statement showing a firm's cash receipts and cash payments during a specified period.

Statement-of-Cash-Flows Method

A method of cash budgeting that is organized along the lines of the statement of cash flows.

Statement of condition

A document describing the status of assets, liabilities, and equity of a person or business at a particular time.

Statement of Financial Accounting Standards No. 8

The is a currency translation standard once used by U.S. accounting firms. See: Statement of Accounting Standards No. 52.

Statement of Financial Accounting Standards No. 52

The currency translation standard currently used by

US firms. It mandates the use of the current rate method. See: Statement of Financial Accounting Standards No. 8.

"Static" Return

The return that an investor would make on a particular position if the underlying stock were unchanged in price at the expiration of the options in the position.

Static theory of capital structure

Theory that the firm's capital structure is determined by a trade-off of the value of tax shields against the costs of bankruptcy.

Stationary time series

A longitudinal measure in which the process generating returns is identical over time.

Statistical Arbitrage

In the context of hedge funds, a style of management that employs complex statistical models that try to capture small abnormalities in a security's intraday return.

Statistical tracking error

Used in the context of general equities. Standard deviation of the difference between the portfolio return and the desired investment benchmark return.

State tax-exempt income fund

A mutual fund that seeks current income exempt from federal and a specific state's income taxes.

State Trading Enterprises

STEs are entities established by governments to import, export and/or produce certain products. Examples include: government-operated import/export monopolies and marketing boards or private companies that receive special or exclusive privileges from their governments to engage in trading activities.

Statistical Office of the European Community

EUROSTAT provides European Economic Community-wide statistics on economics, finance, foreign trade, services, transportation, industry, population, social conditions, energy, agricultural, forestry, and other topics. Eurostat offices are located in Luxembourg.

Statutory debt limit

The cap that Congress imposes on the amount of public debt that may be outstanding whether temporary or permanent. When this limit is reached, the Treasury may not sell new debt issues until Congress raises the limit. For a detailed listing of changes in the limit since 1941, see Budget of the United States Government. See: Debt outstanding subject to limitation.

Statutory investment

An investment that a trustee is authorized to make under state law.

Statutory merger

A merger in which one corporation remains as a legal entity, instead of a new legal entity being formed.

Statutory surplus

The surplus of an insurance company determined by the accounting treatment of both assets and liabilities as established by state statutes.

Statutory voting

The standard rule in most corporations that there is one vote per share in elections of the board of directors.

Staying power

The ability of an investor to stay in the market and not to sell out of a position when an investment has fallen in value.

STD

The ISO 4217 currency code for the Sao Tome & Principe Dobra.

Steady state

As an MBS pool ages, or four to six months after component mortgages have passed at least once the threshold for refinancing, the prepayment speed tends to stabilize within a fairly steady range.

Steamship Conference

A group of steamship operators that operate under mutually agreed-upon freight rates.

Steenth

1/16 (0.0625) of one full point in price. Often used in negotiations to compromise an eighth difference, and in options trading.

Steepening of the yield curve

A change in the yield curve where the spread between the yield on a long-term and short-term Treasury has increased. Compare flattening of the yield curve and butterfly shift.

Step aside

Allow a block to trade at a price at which you do not care to participate in the trade.

Step-down note

A floating-rate note whose interest rate declines after a specified period of time.

Step up

To increase, as in step up the tax basis of an asset.

Step-up bond

A bond that pays a lower coupon rate for an initial period, and then increases to a higher coupon rate. Related: Deferred-interest bond, payment-in-kind bond.

Step-up swap

An interest rate swap on which the notional principal increases according to a predetermined schedule.

Sterilized intervention

Foreign exchange market activity by which monetary authorities insulate their domestic money supplies from the foreign exchange transactions with offsetting sales or purchases of domestic assets.

Sticky deal

A new securities issue that may be difficult to sell because of problems in the market or underlying problems with the corporation.

Stochastic models

Liability-matching models that assume that the liability payments and the asset cash flows are uncertain. Related: Deterministic models.

Stochastics index

A computerized tool measuring overbought and oversold conditions in a stock over a certain period.

Stock

Ownership of a corporation indicated by shares, which represent a piece of the corporation's assets and earnings.

Stock ahead

When two or more orders for a stock at a certain price arrive about the same time, and the exchange's priority rules take effect. NYSE rules stipulate that the bid made first should be executed first, or, if two bids come in at once, the bid for the larger number of shares receives priority. The bid that is not executed is then turned to the broker, who informs the customer that the trade was not completed because there was "stock ahead.".

Stock bonus plan

A plan used as an incentive that rewards employee performance with stock in the company.

Stockbroker

See: Registered representative.

Stock Appreciation Right (SAR)

A contractual right, often granted in tandem with an option that allows an individual to receive cash or stock of a value equal to the appreciation of the stock from the grant date to the date the SAR is exercised.

Stock buyback

A corporation's purchase of its own outstanding stock, usually in order to raise the company's earnings per share.

Stock certificate

A document representing the number of shares of a corporation owned by a shareholder.

Stock dividend

Payment of a corporate dividend in the form of stock rather than cash. The stock dividend may be additional shares in the company, or it may be shares in a subsidiary being spun off to shareholders. Stock dividends are often used to conserve cash needed to operate the business. Unlike a cash dividend, stock dividends are not taxed until sold.

Stock Exchange Automated Quotation System (SEAQ)

London's Nasdaq system.

Stock Exchange of Hong Kong (SEHK)

Only stock exchange located in Hong Kong.

Stock Exchange, Mumbai (BSE)

Formerly the Bombay stock exchange, the BSE accounts for more than one-third of Indian trading volume.

Stock Exchange of Singapore (SES)

The only stock exchange in Singapore.

Stock Exchange of Thailand

The major securities market of Thailand.

Stock exchanges

Formal organizations, approved and regulated by the Securities and Exchange Commission (SEC), that are made up of members who use the facilities to exchange certain common stocks. The two major national stock exchanges are the New York Stock Exchange (NYSE) and the American Stock Exchange (ASE or AMEX). Five regional stock exchanges include the Midwest, Pacific, Philadelphia, Boston, and Cincinnati. The Arizona Stock Exchange is an after-hours electronic marketplace where anonymous participants trade stocks via personal computers.

Stock index

Index like the Dow Jones Industrial Average that tracks a portfolio of stocks.

Stock Index Future

A security that uses composite stock indexes to allow investors to speculate on the performance of the entire market, or to hedge against losses in long or short positions. The settlement of the contracts is in cash.

Stock index option

An option in which the underlying is a common stock index.

Stock index swap

A swap involving a stock index. The other asset involved in a stock index swap can be another stock index (a stock-for-stock swap), a debt index (a debt-for-stock swap), or any other financial asset or financial price index.

Stock insurance company

An insurance company owned by a group of stockholders, who are not necessarily policyholders.

Stock jockey

A stock broker who frequently buys and sells shares in a client's portfolios.

Stock list

The department within a stock exchange that oversees compliance with listing requirements and exchange regulations.

Stock market

Also called the equity market, the market for trading equities.

Stock option

An option whose underlying asset is the common stock of a corporation.

Stock power

A power of attorney form giving ownership of a security to another person, brokerage firm, bank, or lender after it has been sold or pledged to that party.

Stock purchase plan

A plan allowing employees of a company to purchase shares of the company, often at a discount or with matching employer funds.

Stock rating

An evaluation by a rating agency of the expected financial performance or inherent risk of common stocks.

Stock record

The accounting a brokerage firm keeps of all securities held in inventory.

Stock replacement strategy

A strategy for enhancing a portfolio's return, used when the futures contract is expensive according to its theoretical price. The strategy involves a swap between the futures and a Treasury bill and stock portfolio.

Stock repurchase

A firm's repurchase of outstanding shares of its common stock.

Stock right

Another terminology for a stock option.

Stock selection

An active portfolio management technique that focuses on advantageous selection of particular stock rather than on broad asset allocation choices.

Stock split

Occurs when a firm issues new shares of stock and in turn lowers the current market price of its stock to a level that is proportionate to pre-split prices. For example, if IBM trades at $100 before a two-for-one split, after the split it will trade at $50, and holders of the stock will have twice as many shares as they had before the split. See: Split.

Stock symbol

See: Ticker symbol.

Stock ticker

A letter designation assigned to securities and mutual funds that trade on US financial exchanges.

StockWatch

A stock surveillance program offered by proxy solicitation firms, and selected transfer agents, to track and monitor sales and purchases of a corporation's shares and provide valuable information at the beneficial owner level.

Stock watcher (NYSE)

A computerized service that monitors and investigates trading activity on the NYSE in order to identify any unusual activity or security movement that might be caused by rumors or illegal activities.

Stockholder

See: Shareholder.

Stockholder books

Set of books kept by firm management for its annual report that follows Financial Accounting Standards Board rules. The tax books follow IRS tax rules.

Stockholder equity

Balance sheet item that includes the book value of ownership in the corporation. It includes capital stock, paid-in surplus, and retained earnings.

Stockholder of record

Stockholder whose name is registered on the books of a corporation and thus will receive dividends from the corporation.

Stockholder's equity

The residual claims that stockholders have against a firm's assets, calculated by subtracting all current liabilities and debt liabilities from total assets.

Stockholder's report

The annual report and other reports given to stockholders to inform them of the company's financial standing and developments.

Stockholm Stock Market (Stockholm B&#ouml;rsen)

The major securities market of Sweden.

Stockout

Running out of inventory.

Stop basis

Refers to over-the-counter trading. Method of entering an OTC trade into the trader's position without reporting the trade on the OTC tape.

Stop-limit order

A stop order that designates a price limit. Unlike the stop order, which becomes a market order once the stop is reached, the stop-limit order becomes a limit order.

Stop-loss order

An order to unwind a position when the price moves against you. For example, you had purchased a stock, the stop-loss order would be to sell the stock when the price falls to a specified level. If you were short the asset, the stop-loss would trigger a purchase.

Stop order (or stop)

An order to buy or sell at the market when a definite price is reached, either above (on a buy) or below (on a sell) the price that prevailed when the order was given.

Stop-out price

The lowest auction price at which Treasury bills are sold.

Stop payment

An order given a depository institution not to pay out cash for a check; often used when the check has been stolen or lost.

Stop Transfer

A block placed against a security reported lost or stolen (an adverse claim), so it cannot be transferred.

Stopped

Guaranteed a specific price on the customer's working order while the dealer tries to obtain a better one. Stopped against one's self involves a customer order and a firm's own account, not two customers. One can cancel an order even after being stopped by another party.

Stopped out

A purchase or sale that is executed under a stop order at the stop price specified by the customer.

Stopping curve

A curve showing the refunding rates for different times at which the expected value of refunding immediately equals the expected value of waiting to refund.

Stopping curve refunding rate

A refunding rate that falls on the stopping curve.

Story stock/bond

A highly complex security that requires a long "story" so that investors may understand the corporation and be persuaded of its merits.

Straddle

Purchase or sale of an equal number of puts and calls with the same terms at the same time. Related: Spread.

Straight

Direct telephone line, compared to an outside line that requires a telephone number to be dialed.

Straight Bill of Lading

A non-negotiable bill of lading in which the goods are consigned directly to a named consignee.

Straight Discount

The rate applied to the face value of the promissory note to calculate present value without compounding. For example, a note with a face value in three years of 100, with a straight discount of 10% per annum has a present value of 70.

Straight-line depreciation

Amortizing or apportioning an equal dollar amount of depreciation in each accounting period.

Straight term insurance policy

Term life insurance policy providing a fixed-amount death benefit over a certain number of years.

Straight value

Also called investment value, the value of a convertible security without the conversion option.

Straight voting

Allows shareholder to cast all of the shareholder's votes for each candidate for the board of directors.

Strange Attractor

An attractor in phase space, where the points never repeat themselves, and orbits never intersect, but they stay within the same region of phase space. Unlike limit cycles or point attractors, strange attractors are non-periodic, and generally have a fractal dimension. They are a picture of a non-linear, chaotic system. See: Attractor, Chaos, Limit Cycle, Point Attractor.

Strangle

Buying or selling an out-of-the-money put option and call option on the same underlying instrument, with the same expiration. Profits are made only if there is a drastic change in the underlying instrument's price.

Strategic alliance

Collaboration between two or more companies designed to achieve some corporate objective. May include international licensing agreements, management contracts, or joint ventures.

Strategic buyout

Acquisition of another firm in order to realize some operational benefits which will result in increased earnings.

Strategy

The general or specific approach to investing that an individual, institution, or fund manager employs.

Strategic Level of Controls

Commodity groupings used for export control purposes. See: Export Control Classification Number.

Stratified equity indexing

A method of constructing a replicating portfolio that classifies the stocks in the index into strata, and represents each stratum in the portfolio.

Stratified sampling approach to indexing

Dividing an index into cells, each representing a different characteristic of the index, such as duration or maturity.

Stratified sampling bond indexing

A method of bond indexing that divides the index into cells, each cell representing a different characteristic, and that buys bonds to match those characteristics.

Stray

(1) Not a member of the participating party in the trade at hand; (2) not a meaningful indication of a customer's desire to take a sizable position or be involved in a stock.

Street

Means Wall Street financial community; brokers, dealers, underwriters, and other knowledgeable participants.

Street name

Registration under which securities maybe held by a broker on behalf of a client but be registered in the name of the Wall Street firm.

Strike index

For a stock index option, the index value at which the buyer of the option can buy or sell the underlying stock index. The strike index is converted to a dollar value by multiplying by the option's contract multiple. Related: Strike price.

Strike price

The stated price per share for which underlying stock may be purchased (in the case of a call) or sold (in the case of a put) by the option holder upon exercise of the option contract.

Striking price

The price at which an option can be exercised. See: Exercise price.

Striking Price Intercal

The distance between striking prices on a particular underlying security. Normally, the interval is 2-1/2 points for stocks under $25, 5 points for stocks selling over $25 per share, and 10 points (or greater) is acceptable for stocks over $200 per share. There are, however, exceptions to this general guideline.

Strip

Variant of a straddle. A strip is two puts and one call on a stock. A strap is two calls and one put on a stock. The puts and calls have the same strike price and expiration date. See: Strap.

Strip mortgage participation certificate (strip PC)

Ownership interests in specified mortgages purchased by Freddie Mac from a single seller in exchange for separate instruments representing interests in the same mortgages.

Stripped bond

Bond that can be subdivided into a series of zero-coupon bonds.

Stripped mortgage-backed securities (SMBS)

Securities that redistribute the cash flows from the underlying generic MBS collateral into the principal and interest components of the MBS to enhance their attractiveness to different groups of investors.

Stripped yield

Applies mainly to convertible securities. Return on the debt portion of a bond/warrant unit after subtracting the value of the issued warrant segment.

Strong Currency

A currency whose value compared to other currencies is improving, as indicated by a decrease in the direct exchange rates for the currency.

Strong dollar

When the dollar can be exchanged for a large amount of foreign currency, benefiting travelers but hurting exporters.

Strong-form efficiency

A form of pricing efficiency, that posits that the price of a security reflects all information, whether or not it is publicly available. Related: Weak-form efficiency, semi-strong form efficiency.

Strong form of the EMT

Theory that market prices reflect all relevant publicly and privately available information. Defined by Eugene F. Fama in 1970.

Structural Adjustment Loan Facility (SAL)

World Bank program established in 1980 to enhance a country's long-term economic growth through financing projects.

Structural Impediments Initiative

The SII was started in July 1989 to identify and solve structural problems that restrict bringing two-way trade between the U.S. and Japan into better balance.

Structured arbitrage transaction

A self-funding, self-hedged series of transactions that usually use mortgage-backed securities (MBS) as the primary assets.

Structured Asset Trust Unit Repackagings

A synthetic security linked or weak-linked to underlying collateral. Ratings usually reflect the credit quality of the underlying securities.

Structured debt

Debt that has been customized for the buyer, often by incorporating unusual options.

Structured note

A derivative investment that will change in value with movements of an underlying index; or a note whose issuer makes swap arrangements to alter its required cash flows.

Structured portfolio strategy

Designing a portfolio to achieve a level of performance that matches some predetermined liabilities that must be paid out in the future.

Structured settlement

An agreement in settlement of a lawsuit involving specific payments made over a period of time. Property and casualty insurance companies often buy life insurance products to pay the costs of such settlements.

Stub

Often used in risk arbitrage. Piece of equity security left over from a major cash or security distribution from a recapitalization.

Student Loan Marketing Association (SLMA)

A publicly traded corporation established by federal action that increases availability of educational loans by guaranteeing student loans traded in the secondary market. Also known as Sallie Mae.

Subchapter M

An IRS regulation dealing with investment companies and real estate investment trusts that avoid double taxation by distributing interest, dividends, and capital gains directly to shareholders, who are taxed individually.

Subchapter S

IRS regulation that gives a corporation with 35 or fewer shareholders the option of being taxed as a partnership to escape corporate income taxes.

Subcontractor production

Overseas production of a part or component of a U.S.-origin article. The subcontract does not necessarily involve license of technical information and is usually a direct commercial arrangement between the U.S. manufacturer and a foreign producer.

Subject

Refers to a bid or offer that cannot be executed without confirmation from the customer. In other words, not firm, but a bid/offer that needs additional information/confirmation before becoming firm and is therefore still negotiable.

Subject market

Quote in which prices are subject to confirmation. See: Fast market.

Subject to a (NY) can

Contingent upon trader's ability to cancel an order (on the indicated exchange).

Subject to opinion

An auditor's opinion reflecting acceptance of a company's financial statements subject to pervasive uncertainty that cannot be adequately measured, such as information relating to the value of inventories, reserves for losses, or other matters open to judgment.

Subject to a print/execution/trading

Contingent on execution of a trade because the picture in the stock has not been materially altered.

Subjective probabilities

Probabilities that are determined subjectively (for example, on the basis of judgment rather than statistical sampling).

Subordinated

A claim ranked lower in priority than other claims. Common stock claims are always subordinated to debt.

Subordinated bonds

Securities that fall after others in priority of claims on the entity in the case of financial distress.

Subordinated debenture bond

An unsecured bond that ranks after secured debt, after debenture bonds, and often after some general creditors in its claim on assets and earnings. Related: Debenture bond, mortgage bond, collateral trust bonds.

Subordinated debt

Debt over which senior debt takes priority. In the event of bankruptcy, subordinated debtholders receive payment only after senior debt claims are paid in full.

Subordination clause

A provision in a bond indenture that restricts the issuer's future borrowing by subordinating future lenders' claims on the firm to those of the existing bondholders.

Subpart F

Special category of foreign-source "unearned" income that is currently taxed by the IRS whether or not it is remitted to the US

Subperiod return

The return of a portfolio over a shorter period of time than the evaluation period.

Subrogation

The operation by which the insurance company (on payment of a claim) assumes all of the assured's rights to recovery from any third parties; substitution of one creditor for another.

Subscription

Agreement to buy new issue of securities.

Subscription agreement

An application reviewed by the general partner to join a limited partnership.

Subscription price

Price that current shareholders pay for a share of stock in a rights offering.

Subscription privilege

The right of current shareholders of a corporation to buy newly issued shares before they are available to the public.

Subscription right

See: Subscription privilege.

Subscription warrant

Applies to derivative products. Type of security, usually issued with another security, such as a bond or stock, that entitles the holder to buy a proportionate amount of common stock at a specified price, usually higher than the market price at the time of issuance. Warrant.

Subsidiary

A wholly or partially owned company that is part of a large corporation. A foreign subsidiary is a separately incorporated entity under the host country's law. A subsidiary's financial results are carried on the parent company's books.

Subsidies

GATT does not directly define subsidies. The U.S. regards a subsidy as a bounty or grant paid for the manufacture, production, or export of an article. Export subsidies are contingent on exports; domestic subsidies are conferred on production without reference to exports. While governments sometimes make outright payments to firms; subsidies usually take a less direct form (R&D support, tax breaks, loans on preferential terms, and provision of raw materials at below-market prices).

Subsidized financing

Funding provided by a government or other entity that is available at a below-market interest rate.

Substitute sale

A method for hedging price risk that uses debt market instruments, such as interest rate futures, or that involves selling borrowed securities as the primary assets.

Substitution swap

A swap in which a money manager exchanges one bond for another bond that is similar in terms of coupon, maturity, and credit quality, but that offers a higher yield.

Substantially equal periodic payments (SEPP)

A method of distribution from IRA account assets that under certain conditions is not subject to the IRS's 10% premature withdrawal penalty for those under age 59-1/2.

Success tax

A 15% excise tax on "excess" distributions from tax-deferred retirement plans that was repealed by the Taxpayer Relief Act of 1997. In essence, the tax had penalized "successful" investors who accumulated large retirement accounts and took distributions that exceeded an annual limit deemed excessive by the tax code.

Suicide pill

A hostile takeover prevention tactic that could destroy the target company. Taking on a large amount of debt to prevent the takeover might cause bankruptcy, for example.

Suitability

A requirement that any investing strategy fall within the financial means and investment objectives of an investor.

Suitability rules

Policies and guidelines that brokers must use to ensure that investors have the financial means to assume risks that they wish to undertake. These are enforced by the NASD and other self-regulatory organizations.

Suitable

Describing a strategy or trading philosophy in which the investor is operating in accordance with his(her) financial means and investment objectives.

Summary Investigation

A 20-day investigation conducted by the International Trade Administration immediately following filing of an antidumping petition to ascertain if the petition contains sufficient information with respect to sales at "less than fair value" and the injury or threat of material injury to a domestic industry caused by the alleged sales at "less than fair value" to warrant the initiation of an antidumping investigation. See: Tariff Act of 1930.

Summary plan description (SPD)

A document that explains the fundamental features of an employer's defined benefit or defined contribution plan, including eligibility requirements, contribution formulas, vesting schedules, benefit calculations, and distribution options. ERISA requires that the SPD be easy to understand and that each participant receive a copy within 90 days of joining the plan.

Summit Conference

A summit conference is an international meeting at which heads of government are the chief negotiators, major world powers are represented, and the meeting serves substantive rather than ceremonial purposes.

The term first came into use in reference to the Geneva Big Four Conference of 1955.

Sum-of-the-years'-digits depreciation

Method of accelerated depreciation.

Sunflowerseed Oil Assistance Program

SOAP, one of four export subsidy programs operated by the Department of Agriculture, helps U.S. exporters meet prevailing world prices for sunflowerseed oil in targeted markets. USDA pays cash to U.S. exporters as bonuses, making up the difference between the higher U.S. cost of acquiring sunflowerseed oil and the lower world price at which it is sold.

Sunk costs

Costs that have been incurred and cannot be reversed.

Sunrise industries

Growth industries in an economy that may become leaders in the market in the future.

Super Bowl indicator

A theory that if a team from the old American Football League pre-1970 wins the Super Bowl, the stock market will decline during the coming year. If a team from the old pre-1990 National Football League wins the Super Bowl, stock prices will increase in the coming year.

Super DOT

Super DOT provides faster execution than regular DOT and focuses on large-size trades and baskets. See: Program trading.

Super Majority

A proposal requiring more than a simple majority of the votes eligible to be cast at an annual or special meeting. A super majority is often a 2/3 (66.66%) vote, but it can be as high as 3/4 (75%) or 4/5 (80%).

Super message

See: Autex.

Super sinker bond

Usually a home financing bond, but also any other bond that has long-term coupons but short maturity; the mortgages may be prepaid, and the holders may receive the long-term yield after a short period of time.

Supermajority

Provision in a company's charter requiring a majority of, say, 80% of shareholders to approve certain changes, such as a merger.

Supermajority amendment

Often used in risk arbitrage. Corporate amendment requiring that a substantial majority (usually 67% to 90%) of stockholders approve important transactions, such as mergers.

Supervisory analyst

An analyst who is qualified to approve publicly distributed research reports on the NYSE.

Supervisory board

The board of directors that represents stakeholders in the governance of the corporation.

Supplemental Security Income

A Social Security program established to help the blind, disabled, and poor.

Supplier Credit

Credits granted by a supplier, usually through commercial banks, to a foreign buyer under deferred payment terms.

Supply Access

Assurances that importing countries will, in the future, have fair and equitable access at reasonable prices to supplies of raw materials and other essential imports. Such assurances should include explicit constraints against the use of the export embargo as an instrument of foreign policy.

Supply shock

An event that influences production capacity and costs in an economy.

Supply-side economics

A theory of economics that reductions in tax rates will stimulate investment and in turn will benefit the entire society.

Support

An effective lower bound on prices supported because of many willing buyers at that price level.

Support for East European Democracy

The SEED Act, signed into law in November 1989, contained 25 distinct actions to support structural adjustment, private sector development, trade and investment, and educational, cultural, and scientific activities in Poland and Hungary. Funding for most of the actions was provided by the Agency for International Development. The SEED Act expired at the end of fiscal year 1990. Since then support has been provided under the Foreign Assistance Act of 1991. See: Foreign Assistance Act of 1991.

Support level

A price level below which it is supposedly difficult for a security or market to fall. That is, the price level at which a security tends to stop falling because there is more demand than supply; can be identified on a technical basis by seeing where the stock has bottomed out in the past.

Surcharge

An additional levy added to some charge.

Surety

An individual or corporation that guarantees the performance or actions of another.

Surplus funds

Cash flow available after payment of taxes in a project.

Surplus management

Related: Asset management.

Surtax

A tax added to the normal tax paid by corporations or individuals who have earned income above a certain level.

Surveillance department of exchanges

A department that monitors trading activity on an exchange in order to identify any unusual activity that may indicate illegal practices.

Surveyor

A marine specialist who examines damaged property and determines the cause, nature, and extent of damage and methods of repair and/or replacement. He is not an adjuster, and all his actions are without prejudice to policy terms and conditions.

Survivorship bias

Usually pertaining to fund manager or individual investor performance. Suppose we examined the performance over the last ten years of a group of managers that exist today. This performance is biased upwards because we are only considering those that survived for 10 years. That is, some dropped out because of poor performance. Hence, in evaluating performance, one has to be careful to include both the current and the managers that dropped out of the sample due to poor performance.

Sushi bond

A Eurobond issued by a Japanese corporation.

Suspended trading

Temporary halt in trading in a particular security, in advance of a major news announcement or to correct an imbalance of orders to buy and sell.

Suspense account

An account used temporarily to record receipts and disbursements that have yet to be classified.

Suspension of Investigation

A decision to suspend an antidumping investigation if the exporters who account for substantially all of the imported merchandise agree to stop exports to the U.S. or agree to revise their prices promptly to eliminate any dumping margin. An investigation may be suspended at any time before a final determination is made. No agreement to suspend an investigation may be made unless effective monitoring of the agreement is practicable and is determined to be in the public interest. See: Tariff Act of 1930.

Suspension of Liquidation

If affirmative, the preliminary determination of dumping or subsidization, or final determination after a negative preliminary determination, provides for suspension of liquidation of all entries of merchandise subject to the determination which are entered, or withdrawn from warehouse, for consumption, on or after the date of the publication of the notice in the Federal Register. Customs is directed to require a cash deposit, or the posting of a bond or other security, for each entry affected equal to the estimated amount of the subsidy or the amount by which the fair value exceeds the U.S. price. When an administrative review is completed, Customs is directed to collect the final subsidy rate or amount by which the foreign market value exceeds the U.S. price, and to require for each entry thereafter a cash deposit equal to the newly determined subsidy rate or margin of dumping. See: Tariff Act of 1930.

Sustainable growth rate

Maximum rate of growth a firm can sustain without increasing financial leverage.

SV

The two-character ISO 3166 country code for EL SALVADOR.

SVC

The ISO 4217 currency code for the El Salvador Colon.

Swap

An arrangement in which two entities lend to each other on different terms, e.g., in different currencies, and/or at different interest rates, fixed or floating.

Swap arrangements

Short-term reciprocal lines of credit between the Federal Reserve and 14 foreign centeral banks as well as the Bank for International Settlements. Through a swap transaction, the Federal Reserve can, in effect, borrow foreign currency in order to purchase dollars in the foreign exchange market. In doing so, the demand for dollars and the dollar's foreign exchange value are increased. Similarly, the Federal Reserve can temporarily provide dollars to foreign central banks through swap arrangments.

Swap assignment

Related: Swap sale.

Swap book

A swap bank's portfolio of swaps, usually arranged by currency and maturity.

Swap buy back

The sale of an interest rate swap by one counterparty to the other, effectively ending the swap.

Swap fund

See: Exchange fund.

Swap Network

The swap network is a series of bilateral arrangements between the Federal Reserve and fourteen foreign central banks and the Bank for International Settlements providing standby reciprocal facilities for obtaining foreign currencies. The facilities provide for the swap (simultaneous spot purchase and forward sale) of each other's currency by the Federal Reserve and the respective foreign central bank. Swap drawings typically have a three-month maturity, with an understanding that they may be more or less automatically rolled over for another three months.

Swap option

See: Swaption. Related: Quality option.

Swap rate

The difference between spot and forward rates expressed in points, e.g., \$0.0001 per pound sterling.

Swap reversal

An interest rate swap designed to end a counterparty's role in another interest rate swap, accomplished by counterbalancing the original swap in maturity, reference rate, and notional amount.

Swaps

Swaps take dozens of forms but often entail the exchange of one type of asset or payment for another. Some of the more common forms are: cross-border; currency; debt-for-charity; debt-for-commodity; debt-for-debt; debt-for-development; debt-for-equity; debt-for-export; debt-for-local-currency; debt-for-nature; discount; dual currency; interest rate; inward; premium; reverse; and vanilla. Minor variation in names is common.

Currency swaps convert principal from the lender's currency into the debtor's currency and receiving interest payments in the debtor's currency. The swap, made to protect the principal from future changes in foreign exchange rates, involves a forward exchange contract to recover the currency involved.

Debt swaps entail replacing the foreign liabilities of a debtor country with ownership or rights of value. A debt-for-equity swap replaces foreign liabilities with a stake in the debtor country's national enterprises; a debt-for-export swap replaces foreign liabilities with an arrangement to receive proceeds from the overseas sale of the debtor country's products or commodities; a debt-for-debt swap replaces an existing foreign liability with a new commitment from the debtor country.

Interest rate swaps involve agreements on the means for exchanging future cash flows. Single currency interest rate swaps concern exchanging future cash flow in the same currency and offer a means for modifying the impact of future changes in interest rates on a company's profitability. Cross currency interest rate swaps concern exchanging future cash flows between one currency and another, traded either on a fixed or floating rate, and offer a means for limited the risk of converting financial interests between currencies.

Swaps also involve arrangements whereby different sellers of similar commodities swap and deliver them to each other's customer if such action saves transportation costs. See: Derivatives.

Swap sale

Also called a swap assignment, a transaction that ends one counterparty's role in an interest rate swap by substituting a new counterparty whose credit is acceptable to the other original counterparty.

Swaption

Options on interest rate swaps. The buyer of a swaption has the right to enter into an interest rate swap agreement by some specified date in the future. The swaption agreement will specify whether the buyer of the swaption will be a fixed-rate receiver or a fixed-rate payer. The writer of the swaption becomes the counterparty to the swap if the buyer exercises.

Sweat equity

An increase in equity created by the labor of the owner.

Swedish International Development Authority

SIDA, an agency responsible to the Ministry for Foreign Affairs, administers the greater portion of Swedish development cooperation. Swedish development assistance is directed toward five goals: economic growth, economic and social equality, economic and political independence, democratic development, and environmental quality. About 50 percent of Sweden's development assistance is directed toward a limited number of designated "program countries" in Africa, Asia, and Latin America and involves negotiated efforts to integrate external assistance and long-term development strategies. The remaining assistance is allocated to UN agencies, international development banks, and about 90 countries. The Authority was established in 1965; headquarters are in Stockholm, Sweden. See: Swedish International Enterprise Development Corporation.

Swedish International Enterprise Development Corporation SwedeCorp, a government funded under Sweden's aid program, supports enterprise development through joint venture investments in developing countries and in Central and Eastern Europe. The Corporation also encourages the transfer of industiral and commercial knowledge from Sweden to third world countries and promotes exports from developing countries to Sweden. The Corporation was formed in July 1991 based on a reorganization of international industry assistance programs; headquarters are in Stockholm, Sweden. See: Swedish International Development Authority.

Sweep account

Account providing that a bank invest all the excess available funds at the close of each business day for the firm.

Sweetener

A feature of a security that makes it more attractive to potential purchasers.

SWIFT

See: Society for Worldwide Interbank Financial Telecommunications.

Swing

Margin of credit allowed on a bilateral clearing account beyond which all trade exchanges stop and cannot be resumed until the swing imbalance is reduced.

Swingline facility

Bank borrowing facility to provide finance while the firm replaces US commercial paper with eurocommercial paper.

Swiss Electronic Bourse (EBS)

Computer linking system between the former stock exchange trading floors in Zurich, Geneva, and Basel, Switzerland so that trades can be carried out among traders on all three of the trading floors.

Swiss Options and Financial Futures Exchange (SOFFEX)

The Swiss derivatives market with the first fully electronic trading system in the world, now called Eurex Zurich AG.

Swiss Exchange

The major securities market of Switzerland.

Swissy

Slang for the Swiss franc.

Switch Arrangements

A form of countertrade in which unused purchase rights under government-to-government trade (clearing agreements) on unwanted goods received by a firm in a countertrade transaction are sold at a discount to buyers for cash.

Switch order

Order for the purchase (sale) of one stock and the sale (purchase) of another stock at a stipulated price difference. Contingent order, swap.

Switching

Liquidating a position and simultaneously reinstating a position in another futures contract of the same type.

Switching options

A sequence of transactions in which exercise of one option creates one or more additional options. Investment-disinvestment, entry-exit, expansion-contraction, and suspension-reactivation decisions are switching options.

Switch Trading

Trade activities connected with converting bilateral clearing imbalances into convertible currencies through the sale of the clearing imbalance to switch traders at discounted prices. The switch traders then reduce or eliminate the imbalance through import/export transactions that they arrange. The term is also used to denote nonclearing transactions involving triangular or multiple sales of different goods by various brokers. By a series of trades at discounted prices, a primary exporter can convert into hard currency revenues a soft currency payment or a countertraded product hard to market.

SY

The two-character ISO 3166 country code for SYRIAN ARAB REPUBLIC.

Sydney Futures Exchange (SFE)

The derivatives market of Australia.

Symbol

Letters used to identify companies on the consolidated tape and other locations.

Symbol book special

Illiquid, inactively traded stock not familiar market.

Symmetric cash matching

An extension of cash flow matching that allows for the short-term borrowing of funds to satisfy a liability prior to the liability due date, reducing the cost of funding liabilities.

Synchronous data

Information available at the same time. To test option-pricing models, the price of the option and of the underlying should be synchronous and reflect the same moment in the market.

Syndicate

A group of banks that acts jointly, on a temporary basis, to loan money in a bank credit (syndicated credit) or to underwrite a new issue of bonds.

Syndicate manager

See: Managing underwriter

Syndicated Eurocredit loans

Funding provided by a group (or syndicate) of banks in the Eurocredit market.

Syndicated Loan

A large Eurocurrency loan from a group of international banks.

Synergistic effect

A violation of value-additivity in that the value of a combination is greater than the sum of the individual values.

Synergy

Describes a combination whose value is greater than the sum of the separate individual parts.

Synthetic convertible

Combination of usable bonds and warrants (that expire on or after the bonds' maturity) that resembles convertible bond.

Synthetic forward position

A forward position constructed through borrowing in one currency, lending in another currency, and offsetting these transactions in the spot exchange market.

Synthetic Lease

When a company creates a special-purpose entity to arrange for a loan to purchase property, and then leases the property from the entity.The synthetic lease therefore keeps the loan off the company's balance sheet, while the company provides enough income to the special-purpose entity to cover the interest rate on the loan.

Synthetic put

A strategy equivalent in risk to purchasing a put option where an investor sells stock short and buys a call.

Synthetic stock

An option strategy that is equivalent to the underlying stock. A long call and a short put is synthetic long stock. A long put and a short call is sythetic short stock.

Synthetics

Customized hybrid instruments created by blending an underlying price on a cash instrument with the price of a derivative instrument. It is a combination of security holdings that mimics the price movement of another single security (i.e., synthetic call: long position in a stock combined with a put on that position; a protected long sale; synthetic put: short position in a stock combined with a call on that position; a protected short sale).

SYP

The ISO 4217 currency code for the Syrian Pound.

Systematic

Common to all businesses.

Systematic investment plan

An approach involving regular investments in order to take advantage of dollar-cost averaging.

Systematic Return

The part of the return dependent on the benchmark return. We can break excess returns into two components: systematic and residual. The systematic return is the beta times the benchmark excess return.

Systematic risk

Also called undiversifiable risk or market risk.

Systematic risk principle

Only the systematic portion of risk matters in large, well-diversified portfolios. Thus, expected returns must be related only to systematic risks.

Systematic withdrawal plan

A provision of certain mutual funds to pay out to the shareholder specified amounts after specified periods of time.

Systemic Risk

Risk common to a particular sector or country. Often refers to a risk resulting from a particular "system" that is in place, such as the regulator framework for monitoring of financial institutions.

System for Tracking Export License Applications

STELA is a BXA computer-generated voice unit that interfaces with the BXA database: ECASS (Export Control Automated Support System). STELA enables a caller to check on an export license by making a telephone call.

System Noise

See: Dynamical Noise.

SZ

The two-character ISO 3166 country code for SWAZILAND.

SZL

The ISO 4217 currency code for the Swaziland Lilangeni.

T

Fifth letter of a Nasdaq stock symbol indicating that the stock has warrants or rights.

TAA

See: Tactical asset allocation.

Table of Denial Orders

The TDO is a list of individuals and firms that have been disbarred from shipping or receiving U.S. goods or technology. Firms and individuals on the list may be disbarred with respect to either controlled commodities or general destination (across-the-board) exports. The list is published in the Export Administration Regulations.

TABs

See: Tax anticipation bill.

Tabulation Report

A proxy tally report detailing the current quorum and vote figures on each proposal.

TAC bonds

See: Targeted amortization class bond.

Tactical Asset Allocation (TAA)

Portfolio strategy that allows active departures from the normal asset mix according to specified objective measures of value. Often called active management. It involves forecasting asset returns, volatilities, and correlations. The forecasted variables may be functions of fundamental variables, economic variables, or even technical variables.

Tail

(1) The difference between the average price in Treasury auctions and the stopout price. (2) A future money market instrument (one available some period hence) created by buying an existing instrument and financing the initial portion of its life with a term repo. (3) The extreme ends under a probability curve. (4) The odd amount in an MBS pool.

Tailgating

Purchase of a security by a broker after the broker places an order for the same security for a customer. The broker hopes to profit either because of information which the customer has or because the customer's purchase is of sufficient size to affect security prices. This is an unethical practice.

Taiwan Stock Exchange (TSEC)

Established in 1961, the only centralized securities market in Taiwan.

Take

(1) To agree to buy. A dealer or customer who agrees to buy at another dealer's offered price is said to take the offer. (2) Euro bankers speak of taking deposits rather than buying money.

Take a bath

To sustain a loss on either a speculation or an investment.

"Take it down"

Reduce the offering price or hit others' bids to such an extent as to lower the inside market.

Take a flier

To speculate on highly risky securities.

"Take me along"

"Allow me to participate in the side of a particular trade.

Take off

A sharp increase in the price of a stock, or a positive movement of the market as a whole.

Take the offer

Buy stock by accepting a floor broker's (listed) or dealer's (OTC) offer at an agreed-upon volume. Antithesis of hit the bid.

Take-out

A cash surplus generated by the sale of one block of securities and the purchase of another, e.g., selling a block of bonds at 99 and buying another block at 95. Also, a bid made to a seller of a security that is designed (and generally agreed) to take the seller out of the market.

Take-or-pay contract

An agreement that obligates the purchaser to take any product that is offered (and pay the cash purchase price) or pay a specified amount if the product is not taken.

Take a position

To buy or sell short; that is to own or to owe some amount on an asset or derivative security.

Take a powder

Temporarily cancel an order or indication in a stock, while unrepresented interest still exists. See: Back on the shelf, sidelines.

Take a swing

Execute a trade at a price that the trader feels is higher or more risky than would normally be acceptable, in order to gain market share in the institutional arena.

Takedown

The share of securities of each participating investment banker in a new or a secondary offering, or the price at which the securities are distributed to the different members of an underwriting group.

Takeover

General term referring to transfer of control of a firm from one group of shareholders to another group of shareholders. Change in the controlling interest of a corporation, either through a friendly acquisition or an unfriendly, hostile, bid. A hostile takeover (with the aim of replacing current existing management) is usually attempted through a public tender offer.

Takeover target

A company that is the object of a takeover attempt, friendly or hostile.

Take-up fee

A fee paid to an underwriter in connection with an underwritten rights offering or an underwritten forced conversion. Represents compensation for each share of common stock the underwriter obtains and must resell upon the exercise of rights or conversion of bonds.

Takes a call

Requires a phone call to an account in order for a trade to be completed. See: Show me.

Takes price

Requiring some price movement or concession on behalf of the initiating party before a trade can be consummated. See: Price give.

Taking delivery

When the buyer actually assumes possession from a seller of assets agreed upon in a forward contract or a futures contract.

Taking a view

A London expression; means forming an opinion as to where market prices are headed and acting on it.

Tandem programs

Ginnie Mae mortgage funds provided at below-market rates to residential MBS buyers with FHA Section 203 and 235 loans and to developers of multifamily projects with Section 236 loans initially and later with Section 221(d)(4) loans.

Tangible asset

An asset whose value depends on particular physical properties. These include reproducible assets such as buildings or machinery and non-reproducible assets such as land, a mine, or a work of art. Also called real assets. Converse of: Intangible asset

Tangible net worth

Total assets minus intangible assets, which include patents and copyrights, and total liabilities.

Tangibility

Characteristic that an assets can be used as collateral to secure debt.

TANs

See: Tax anticipation notes.

Tape

(1) Service that reports prices and sizes of transactions on major exchanges-ticker tape. (2) Dow Jones and other news wires. See: Consolidated tape.

Tape is late

When the trading volume is so heavy that trades appear on the tape more than a minute behind the timer they actually take place.

Tare Weight

The weight of a container and packing materials without the weight of the goods it contains.

Target cash balance

Optimal amount of cash for a firm to hold, considering the trade-off between the opportunity costs of holding too much cash and the trading costs of holding too little cash.

Target company

Often used in risk arbitrage. Firm chosen as an attractive takeover candidate by a potential acquirer. The acquirer may buy up to 5% of the target's stock without public disclosure, but it must report all transactions and supply other information to the SEC, the exchange the target company is listed on, and the target company itself once the 5% threshold is hit. See: Raider.

Target firm

A firm that is the object of a takeover by another firm.

Target investment mix

The percentage mix of stocks, bonds, and short-term reserves that an investor considers appropriate based on his/her personal objectives, time horizon, risk tolerance, and financial resources.

Target Leverage Ratio

The ratio of the market value of debt to the total market value of the firm that management seeks to maintain.

Target payout ratio

A firm's long-run dividend-to-earnings ratio. The firm's policy is to attempt to pay out a certain percentage of earnings, but it pays a stated dollar dividend and adjusts it to the target as base line increases in earnings occur.

Target price

In the context of takeovers, the price at which an acquirer aims to buy a target firm. In the context of options, the price of the underlying security at which an option will become in the money. In the context of stocks, the price that an investor hopes a stock will reach in a certain time period.

Target zone arrangement

A monetary system under which countries pledge to maintain their exchange rates within a specific margin around agreed-upon, fixed central exchange rates.

Target zones

Implicit boundaries on exchange rates established by central banks.

Targeted registered offerings

Securities issues sold to "targeted" foreign financial institutions according to U.S. Securities and Exchange Commission guidelines. These foreign institutions then maintain a secondary market in the foreign market.

Targeted repurchase

Buying back of a firm's stock from a potential acquirer,

usually at a substantial premium, to forestall a takeover attempt. Related: Greenmail.

Targeted Amortization Class (TAC) bonds

Bonds offered as a tranche class of some CMOs, according to a sinking fund schedule. They differ from PAC bonds whose amortization is guaranteed as long as prepayments on the underlying mortgages do not exceed certain limits. A TAC's schedule is met at only one prepayment rate.

Tariff

A tax assessed by a government in accordance with its tariff schedule on goods as they enter (or leave) a country. May be imposed to protect domestic industries from imported goods and/or to generate revenue. Types include ad valorem, specific, variable, or some combination.

Tariff Act of 1930

Title VII of the Tariff Act of 1930, as amended, provides for the imposition of antidumping duties on imported merchandise found to have been sold in the United States at "less than fair value," if these sales have caused or are likely to cause material injury to, or materially retard the establishment of, an industry in the United States.

Tariff Anomaly

A tariff anomaly exists when the tariff on raw materials or semi-manufactured goods is higher than the tariff on the finished product.

Tariff Escalation

A situation in which tariffs on manufactured goods are relatively high, tariffs on semi-processed goods are moderate, and tariffs on raw materials are nonexistent or very low.

Tariff Quotas

Application of a higher tariff rate to imported goods after a specified quantity of the item has entered the country at a lower prevailing rate.

Tariff Schedule

A comprehensive list of the goods which a country may import and the import duties applicable to each product.

Tariff Schedules of the United States

See: Tariff Schedules of the United States Annotated.

Tariff Schedules of the United States Annotated

Effective 1979 to January 1989, the U.S. import statistics were initially collected and compiled in terms of the commodity classifications in the Tariff Schedules of the United States Annotated (TSUSA), an official publication of the U.S. International Trade Commission embracing the legal text of the Tariff Schedules of the United States (TSUS) together with statistical annotations. This publication was superseded by the Harmonized Tariff Schedule of the United States Annotated for Statistical Reporting Purposes (HTSUSA) in January 1989.

Effective 1979 to January 1989, the U.S. export statistics were initially collected and compiled in terms of the commodity classifications in Schedule B, Statistical Classification of Domestic and Foreign Commodities Exported from the United States. Schedule B is a U.S. Bureau of the Census publication and, during this period, was based on the framework of the TSUS. In January 1989, this publication was replaced by Schedule B based on the Harmonized System. See: Schedule B.

Taxable acquisition

A merger or consolidation that is not a tax-fee acquisition. The selling shareholders are treated as having sold their shares.

Taxable equivalent yield

The return from a higher-paying but taxable investment that would equal the return from a tax-free investment. This depends on the investor's tax bracket.

Taxable estate

That portion of a deceased person's estate that is subject to transfer tax.

Taxable event

An event or transaction that has a tax consequence, such as the sale of stock holding that is subject to capital gains taxes.

Taxable income

Gross income less a variety of deductions.

Taxable municipal bond

Taxed private-purpose bonds issued by the state or local government to finance prohibited projects such as sports stadiums.

Taxable transaction

Any transaction that is not tax-free to the parties involved, such as a taxable acquisition.

Taxable year

The 12-month period an individual uses to report income for income tax purposes. For most individuals, their tax year is the calendar year.

Tax anticipation bills (Tabs)

Special bills that the Treasury occasionally issues that mature on corporate quarterly income tax dates and can be used at face value by corporations to pay their tax liabilities.

Tax Anticipation Notes (Tans)

Notes issued by states or municipalities to finance current operations in anticipation of future tax receipts.

Tax arbitrage

Trading that takes advantage of a difference in tax rates or tax systems as the basis for profit.

Tax audit

Audit by the IRS or other tax-collecting agency to determine whether a taxpayer has paid the correct amount of tax.

Tax avoidance

Minimizing tax burden through legal means such as tax-free municipal bonds, tax shelters, IRA accounts, and trusts. Compare with tax evasion.

Tax base

The assessed value of the taxable property, assets, and income within a specific geographic area.

Tax basis

In the context of finance, the original cost of an asset less depreciation that is used to determine gains or losses for tax purposes.

In the context of investments, the price of a stock or bond plus the broker's commission.

Tax books

Records kept by a firm's management that follow IRS rules. The books follow Financial Accounting Standards Board rules.

Tax bracket

The percentage of tax obligation for a particular taxable income.

Tax clawback agreement

An agreement to contribute as equity to a project the value of all previously realized project-related tax benefits not already clawed back. Exercised to the extent required to cover any cash deficiency of the project.

Tax clientele

Categories of investors who have specific preferences for debt or equity because of differences in their personal tax rates.

Tax credit

A direct dollar-for-dollar reduction in tax allowed for expenses such as child care and R&D for building low-income housing. Compare tax deduction.

Tax-deductible

The effect of creating a tax deduction, such as charitable contributions and mortgage interest.

Tax deduction

An expense that a taxpayer is allowed to deduct from taxable income.

Tax-deferred income

Dividends, interest, and unrealized capital gains on investments in an account such as a qualified retirement plan, where income is not subject to taxation until a withdrawal is made.

Tax deferral option

Allowing the capital gains tax on an asset to be payable only when the gain is realized by selling the asset.

Tax-deferred retirement plans

Employer-sponsored and other plans that allow contributions and earnings to be made and accumulate tax-free until they are paid out as benefits.

Tax differential view (of dividend policy)

The view that shareholders prefer capital gains over dividends, and hence low payout ratios, because capital gains are effectively taxed at lower rates than dividends.

Tax Equity and Fiscal Responsibility Act of 1982 (TEFRA)

Legislation to increase tax revenue by eliminating various taxation loopholes and instituting tougher enforcement procedures in collecting taxes.

Tax-equivalent yield

The pre-tax yield required from a taxable bond in order to equal the tax-free yield of a municipal bond.

Tax evasion

Illegal by reducing tax burden by underreporting income, overstating deductions, or using illegal tax shelters.

Tax-exempt bond

A bond usually issued by municipal, county, or state governments whose interest payments are not subject to federal and, in some cases, state and local income tax.

Tax-exempt income

Dividends and interest not subject to federal and, in some cases, state and local income taxes.

Tax-exempt income fund

A mutual fund that seeks income that is exempt from

federal and, in some cases, state and local income taxes.

Tax-exempt money market fund

A money market fund that invests in short-term tax-exempt municipal securities.

Tax-exempt sector

The municipal bond market where state and local governments raise funds. Bonds issued in this sector are exempt from federal income taxes.

Tax-exempt security

An obligation whose interest is tax-exempt, often called a municipal bond, offered by a country, state, town, or any political district.

Tax free acquisition

A merger or consolidation in which (1) the acquirer's tax basis on each asset whose ownership is transferred in the transaction is generally the same as the acquiree's, and (2) each seller who receives only stock does not have to pay any tax on the gain realized until the shares are sold.

Tax haven

A nation with a moderate level of taxation and/or liberal tax incentives for undertaking specific activities such as exporting or investing.

Tax haven affiliate

A wholly owned entity in a low-tax jurisdiction that is used to channel funds to and from a multinational's foreign operations. The tax benefits of tax haven affiliates were largely removed in the US by the Tax Reform Act of 1986.

Tax holiday

A reduced tax rate that a government provides as an inducement to foreign direct investment.

Tax Information Exchange Agreement

A TIEA imposes on the agreeing countries a mutual and reciprocal obligation to exchange information relating to the enforcement of their respective tax laws. A TIEA provides a means by which a signatory government can pursue certain tax evaders, particularly in cases involving large tax claims or drug enforcement. Countries that sign a TIEA agree to: (a) exchange tax information at the government level in a form admissable to U.S. or host country courts; (b) collect information without regard to the taxpayer's nationality; (c) establish a means for compelling the production of tax information; and (d) ensure that local laws do not prohibit the sharing of tax information. A TIEA can support tourism in a signatory country because the Agreement facilitates Internal Revenue Service approval of the destination as a necessary business expense (deductible for Federal income tax purposes) for U.S. citizens and companies which seek to justify attendance at business conventions and seminars in a signatory country.

Tax liability

The amount in taxes a taxpayer to the government.

Tax lien

The right of the government to enforce a claim against the property of a person owing taxes.

Tax and loan account

An account at a private bank, held in the name of the district Federal Reserve Bank, which holds operating cash for the business of the US Treasury.

Tax loss carryback, carryforward

A tax benefit that allows business losses to be used to reduce tax liability in previous and or following years.

Tax-neutrality

Characteristic that taxes do not interfere with the natural flow of capital toward its most productive use.

Tax planning

Devising strategies throughout the year in order to minimize tax liability, for example, by choosing a tax filing status that is most beneficial to the taxpayer.

Tax preference item

Items that must be included when calculating the alternative minimum tax.

Tax preparation services

Firms that prepare tax returns for a fee.

Tax rate

The percentage of tax paid for different levels of income.

Tax Reduction Strategy

A source of competitive advantage that depends on differences in the tax rates imposed in different locations.

Tax Reform Act of 1976

Legislation aimed at tightening provisions relating to taxation, including changes in the capital gains tax laws.

Tax Reform Act of 1984

Legislation enacted as part of the Deficit Reduction Act of 1984 to reduce the federal budget deficit. Among its provisions are a decrease in the minimum holding period for assets to qualify for long-term capital gains treatment from one year to six months.

Tax Reform Act of 1986

A 1986 law involving a major overhaul of the US tax code.

Tax Reform Act of 1993

See: Revenue Reconciliation Act of 1993.

Tax refund

Money back from the government when too much tax has been paid or withheld from a salary.

Tax schedules

Tax forms used to report itemized deductions, dividend and interest income, profit or loss from a business, capital gains and losses, supplemental income and loss, and self-employment tax.

Tax selling

Selling of securities to realize losses that will offset capital gains and reduce tax liability. See: Wash sale.

Tax shelter

Legal methods taxpayers can use to reduce tax liabilities. An example is the use of depreciation of assets.

Tax-sheltered annuity

A type of retirement plan under Section 403(b) of the Internal Revenue Code that permits employees of public educational organizations or tax-exempt organizations to make before-tax contributions via a salary reduction agreement to a tax-sheltered retirement plan. Employers are also allowed to make direct contributions on behalf of employees.

Tax shield

The reduction in income taxes that results from taking an allowable deduction from taxable income.

Tax software

Computer software designed to assist taxpayers in filling out tax returns and minimizing tax liability.

Tax status election

The decision of the status under which to file a tax return. For example, a corporation may file as a C corporation or an S corporation.

Tax straddle

Technique used in futures and options trading to create tax benefits. For example, an investor with a capital gain takes a position creating an artificial offsetting loss in the current tax year and postponing a gain from the position until the next tax year.

Tax swap

Swapping two similar bonds to receive a tax benefit.

Tax-timing option

The option to sell an asset and claim a loss for tax purposes or not sell the asset and defer the capital gains tax.

Tax umbrella

Tax loss carryforwards from previous business losses that form a tax shelter for profits earned in current and future years.

Taxpayer Relief Act of 1997

Legislation forming part of a larger act designed to balance the federal budget. Some of the legislation's provisions included tax credits for taxpayers supporting children, an increase in the amount that could be excluded from estate taxes, and a lower capital gains tax rate.

TBA

See: To be announced.

TC

The two-character ISO 3166 country code for TURKS AND CAICOS ISLANDS.

TD

The two-character ISO 3166 country code for CHAD.

Tear sheet

A page from an S&P stock that provides information on thousands of stocks, often sent to prospective purchasers.

Teaser rate

A low initial interest rate on an adjustable-rate mortgage to entice borrowers, that is later eliminated and replaced by a market-level rate.

Technical Advisory Committees

The TACs are voluntary groups of industry and government representatives who provide guidance and expertise to Commerce on export control matters, including evaluation of technical issues; worldwide availability, use and production of technology; and licensing procedures related to specific industries. TACs have been set up for: (a) materials (Materials Technical Advisory Committee, MATAC), (b) biotechnology (Biotechnology Technical Advisory Committee, BIOTAC), (c) computer systems (CSTAC), (d) electronics (ETAC) (formerly "semiconductors"), (e) sensors (STAC) (formerly "electronic instrumentation"), (f) materials processing equipment (MPETAC) (formerly "automated manufacturing equipment"), (g) regulations and procedures (RPTAC), (h) telecommunications equipment (TETAC), and (i) transportation and related equipment (TRANSTAC).

Technical analysis

Security analysis that seeks to detect and interpret patterns in past security prices.

Technical analysts

Also called chartists or technicians, analysts who use mechanical rules to detect changes in the supply of and demand for a stock, and to capitalize on the expected change.

Technical Barrier to Trade

According to the Standards Code, a specification which sets forth characteristics or standards a product must meet (such as levels of quality, performance, safety, or dimensions) in order to be imported.

Technical condition of a market

Demand and supply factors affecting price, in particular, the net position, either long or short, of the dealer community.

Technical descriptors

Variables that are used to describe the market in terms of patterns in historical data.

Technical forecasting

A forecasting method that uses historical prices and trends.

Technical Information

Information related to the momentum of a particular variable. In market analysis, technical information is information related to market dynamics and crowd behavior only.

Technical insolvency

Default on a legal obligation of the firm. Technical insolvency occurs when a firm doesn't pay a bill on time.

Technical rally

Short rise in securities or commodities futures prices in the face of a general declining trend. Such a rally may result because investors are bargain hunting or because analysts have noticed a particular support level at which securities usually bounce up. Antithesis of correction.

Technical sign

A short-term trend in the price movement of a security that analysts recognize as significant.

Technician

Related: Technical analysts.

Technology

BXA regulations define technical data as "information of any kind that can be used, or adapted for use, in the design, production, manufacture, utilization, or reconstruction of articles or materials. Technology can be either "tangible" or "intangible." Models, prototypes, blueprints or operating manuals (even if stored on recording media) are examples of tangible technology. Intangible technology consists of technical services, such as training, oral advice, information guidance and consulting.

Technology transfer

This term is used to characterize "the transfer of knowledge generated and developed in one place to another, where is it is used to achieve some practical end." Technology may be transferred in many ways: by giving it away (technical journals, conferences, emigration of technical experts, technical assistance programs); by industrial espionage; or by sale (patents, blueprints, industrial processes, and the activities of multinational corporations).

TED spread

Difference between US Treasury bill rate and Eurodollar rate; used by some traders as a measure of investor/trader anxiety or credit quality.

Teeny

1/16 or 0.0625 of one full point in price. Steenth.

TEFRA (Tax Equity and Fiscal Responsibility Act of 1983)

The law requiring federal income tax withholding on payments of dividend and interest to accounts without a certified tax identification number on file. See: W-9.

Tel Aviv Stock Exchange

Israel's only stock exchange.

Telephone switching

Moving one's assets from one mutual fund or variable annuity to another by telephone.

Temporal method

A currency translation method under which the choice of exchange rate depends on the underlying method of valuation. Assets and liabilities valued at historical cost (market cost) are translated at the historical (current market) rate.

Temporary Assets

That portion of a firm's current assets that fluctuates in response to seasonal or anticipated short-term.

Temporary Financing

The sum of negotiated current liabilities and temporary spontaneous current liabilities.

Temporary Importation under Bond

When an importer makes entry of articles brought into the United States temporarily and claimed to be exempt from duty under Chapter 98, Subchapter XIII, Harmonized Tariff Schedule of the United States, a bond is posted with Customs which guarantees that these items will be exported within a specified time frame (usually within one year from the date of importation). Failure to export these items makes the importer liable for the payment of liquidated damages for breach of the bond conditions. The Temporary Importation under Bond (TIB) is usually twice the amount of duties and other payments the importer would otherwise be required to pay. Merchandise imported under TIB is usually for sales demonstration, testing, or repair.

Temporary investment

A short-term investment, such as a money market fund, Treasury bills, or short-term CD, which is usually held a year or less.

Ten largest holdings

The percentage of a portfolio's total net assets or equity holdings in its ten largest securities positions. As this percentage rises, a portfolio's returns are likely to be more volatile because they are more dependent on the fortunes of fewer companies.

10% guideline

The standard analysts' principle that funded debt over 10% of the assessed valuation of taxable property for a municipality is excessive.

10-K

Annual report required by the SEC each year. Provides a comprehensive overview of a company's state of business. Must be filed within 90 days after fiscal year-end. A 10-Q report is filed quarterly.

10-Q

Quarterly report required by the SEC each quarter. Provides a comprehensive overview of a company's state of business.

1040 form

The standard individual tax return form of the IRS.

1099

A statement sent to the IRS and taxpayers by the payers of dividends and interest and by issuers of taxable original issue discount securities.

1099 B

The tax statement used for reporting proceeds resulting from the sale, redemption or liquidation of shares.

1099 DIV

The tax statement used for reporting dividends paid to registered shareholders.

Ten-Day Rule

The New York Stock Exchange rule permitting member firms (brokers) to vote in favor of management ten days or less before the meeting, provided that the member firm mailed proxy material to beneficial owners at least 15 business days before the meeting. The rule allows many shares to be voted, which would otherwise not be, to reach a quorum, approve the choice of directors and auditors and handle other routine matters. This rule does not apply to banks, their nominees or their depository positions, nor to non-routine proposals such as approval for the corporation to issue more shares.

Tenant

A partial owner of a security, or the holder of some property. See: Lessee.

Tenants by Entireties (TEN ENT)

Joint ownership of property or securities by a husband and wife where, upon the death of one, the property goes to the survivor.

Tenants in common

Account registration in which two or more individuals own a certain proportion of an account. Each tenant's proportion is distributable as part of the owners estate, so that if one of the account holders dies, that owner's heirs are entitled to that proportional share of the account.

Tenbagger

A stock that grows in value ten-fold.

Tender

To offer for delivery against futures.

Tender offer

General offer made publicly and directly to a firm's shareholders to buy their stock at a price well above the current market price.

Tender offer premium

The premium offered above the current market price in a tender offer.

Tenor

The length of time until a loan is due. For example, a loan is taken out with a two year tenor. After one year passes, the tenor of the loan is one year.

Term

The period of time during which a contract is in force.

Term bonds

Bonds whose principal is payable at maturity. Often referred to as bullet-maturity bonds or simply bullet bonds. Related: Serial bonds.

Term certificate

A certificate of deposit with a longer time to maturity.

Term Contract (T.C.)

A contract in which a source or sources of supply are established by competitive bid for a specific period of time, at a predermined unit price.

Term Fed funds

Fed funds sold for a period of time longer than overnight.

Terminal value

The value of a bond at maturity, typically its par value, or the value of an asset (or an entire firm) on some specified future valuation date. Usually, a perpetuity formula is used. For example, suppose we forecast cash flows through year 10. We make an assumption that year 11 and beyond will be no growth (except for inflation). If the cash flow forecast for year 11 is 100, the firm's discount rate is 12%, and inflation is expected to be 2%, we use the formula $V_{10} = CF_{11}$/(disc rate-inflation). Hence, the value is 100/(0.12 - 0.02) that is 1,000. This cash flow needs to be brought back to present value using the formula $1000/(1.12)^{10}$, which is 321.97. Note the importance of the inflation assumption.

Term insurance

Provides a death benefit only, no build up of cash value.

Term life insurance

A contract that provides a death benefit but no cash build up or investment component. The premium remains constant only for a specified term of years, and the policy is usually renewable at the end of each term.

Term loan

A bank loan, typically with a floating interest rate, for a specified amount that matures in between one and ten years, and requires a specified repayment schedule.

Term to maturity

The time remaining on a bond's life, or the date on which the debt will cease to exist and the borrower will have completely paid off the amount borrowed. See: Maturity.

Term premiums

Excess of the yields to maturity on long-term bonds over those of short-term bonds.

Term repo

A repurchase agreement with a term of more than one day.

Terms of Reference

TOR is World Bank parlance referring to the preparation of a description of the assignment for consultants to be selected by borrowers following World Bank procedures.

Terms of Delivery

The part of a sales contract that indicates the point at which title and risk of loss of merchandise pass from the seller to the buyer. See: Incoterms.

Terms of Sale

The invoice is the sales contract between buyer and seller and indicates the Terms of Sale.

Terms of Trade

Terms of trade refers to the economic factors affecting a country's foreign trade in goods and services, such as dependency on foreign sourcing and relative competitiveness in production.

Term structure of interest rates

Relationship between interest rates on bonds of different maturities, usually depicted in the form of a graph often called a yield curve. Harvey shows that inverted term structures (long rates below short rates) have preceded every recession over the past 30 years.

Term trust

A closed-end fund that has a fixed termination or maturity date.

Territorial tax system

A tax system that taxes domestic income but not foreign income. Territorial tax regimes are found in Hong Kong, France, Belgium, and the Netherlands.

Test

The event of a price movement that approaches a support level or a resistance level established earlier by the market. A test is passed if prices do not go below the support or resistance level, and the test is failed if prices go on to new lows or highs.

Testamentary trust

A trust created by a will, that is scheduled to occur after the maker's death.

Textile Surveillance Body

The TSB is an international body which meets in Geneva at the GATT to monitor the Multi-Fiber Arrangement. The TSB receives reports of all textile restrictions and can make recommendations to participants. It can mediate disputes between parties to the MFA but has no binding powers. Membership is balanced between importing and exporting members.

TF

The two-character ISO 3166 country code for FRENCH SOUTHERN TERRITORIES.

TG

The two-character ISO 3166 country code for TOGO.

TH

The two-character ISO 3166 country code for THAILAND.

THB

The ISO 4217 currency code for the Thai Baht.

The Curb

Another name for the American Stock Exchange (AMEX).

The Desk

The trading desk at the Federal REserve Bank of New York through which open market purchases and sales of government and federal agancy securities are made. The desk maintains direct telephone communication with major government securities dealers. A "foreign desk" at the Federal Reserve Bank of New York conducts transactions in the foregin exchange market.

Theoretical futures price

The equilibrium futures price. Also called the fair price.

Theoretical spot rate curve

A curve derived from theoretical considerations as applied to the yields of actually traded Treasury debt securities, because there are no zero-coupon Treasury debt issues with a maturity greater than one year. Like the yield curve, this is a graphic depiction of the term structure of interest rates.

Theoretical value

Applies to derivative products. Mathematically determined value of a derivative instrument as dictated by a pricing model such as the Black-Scholes model.

Theta

The ratio of the change in an option price to the decrease in time to expiration. Also called time decay.

Thin market

A market in which trading volume is low, and consequently bid and asked quotes are wide and the instrument traded is not very liquid. Very little stock to buy or sell. Illiquid.

Thinly traded

Infrequently traded.

Third Country Initiative

The TCI was created to help countries establish an export control system on strategic commodities. Such countries, while not members of CoCom, would establish export control systems that provide levels of protection as close as possible to those provided by CoCom Such systems include: (a) import certifications and delivery verifications, (b) controls over reexports of

CoCom-origin, controlled goods and indigenous exports of CoCom-controlled goods, (c) cooperation in pre-licensing and post-shipment checks, and (d) cooperation on enforcement matters. The United States supports the third country initiative through section 5(k) of the Export Administration Act, which allows it to provide selected non-CoCom countries with the same licensing benefits provided to CoCom members.

Third Country Meat Directive

The TCMD is a regulation by which the European Community controls meat imports based on sanitary requirements. The TCMD requires individual inspection and certification by EC veterinarians of U.S. meat plants wishing to export to the EC.

Third market

Exchange-listed securities trading in the OTC market.

Thirty-day visible supply

The total volume in dollars of municipal bonds with maturities of 13 months or more that should reach the market within 30 days.

Thirty-day wash rule

IRS rule stating that losses on a sale of stock may not be used as tax shelter if equivalent stock is purchased 30 days or less before or after the sale of the stock.

Three-phase DDM

A version of the dividend discount model that applies a different expected dividend rate depending on a company's life-cycle phase: growth phase, transition phase, or maturity phase.

Three steps and a stumble rule

A rule predicting that stock and bond prices will fall following three increases in the discount rate by the

Federal Reserve. This is a result of increased costs of borrowing for companies and the increased attractiveness of money market funds and CDs over stocks and bonds as a result of the higher interest rates.

Threshold for refinancing

The point when the weighted-average coupon of an MBS is at a level to induce homeowners to prepay the mortgage in order to refinance to a lower-rate mortgage, generally reached when the weighted-average coupon of the MBS is 2 percentage points or more above currently available mortgage rates.

Thrift institution

An organization formed as a depository for primarily consumer savings. Savings and loan associations and savings banks are thrift institutions.

Thrift Institution Advisory Council (TIAC)

A council, established following the passage of the Monetary Control Act of 1980, whose purpose is to provide information and views on the special needs and problems of thrifts. The group is comprised of representatives of savings banks, savings and loan associations, and credit unions.

Thrift plan

A defined contribution plan in which an employee contributes, usually on a before-tax basis, toward the ultimate benefits that will be provided. The employer usually agrees to match all or a portion of the employee's contributions.

Through Bill of Lading

A single bill of lading converting both the domestic and international carriage of an export shipment. An air waybill is essentially a through bill of lading used for air shipments. However, ocean shipments usually require two separate documents — an inland B/L for domestic carriage and an ocean B/L for international carriage. Through bills of lading are insufficient for ocean shipments.

Throughput agreement

An agreement to put a specified amount of product per period through a particular facility. An example is an agreement to ship a specified amount of crude oil per period through a particular pipeline.

Tick

Refers to the minimum change in price a security can have, either up or down. Related: Point.

Tick indicator

A market indicator based on the number of stocks whose last trade was an uptick or a downtick. Used as an indicator of market sentiment or psychology to try to predict the market's trend.

Tick-test rules

SEC-imposed restrictions on when a short sale may be executed, intended to prevent investors from destabilizing the price of a stock when the market price is falling. A short sale can be made only when either (1) the sale price of the particular stock is higher than the last trade price (referred to as an uptick trade) or (2) if there is no change in the last trade price of the particular stock, the previous trade price must be higher than the trade price that preceded it (referred to as a zero uptick).

Ticker symbol

An abbreviation assigned to a security for trading purposes.

Ticker tape

Computerized device that relays to investors around the world the stock symbol and the latest price and volume on securities as they are traded.

Ticket

An abbreviation of order ticket.

Tied Aid Credit

Tied aid credit refers to the practice of providing grants and/or concessional loans, either alone or combined with export credits, linked to procurement from the donor country.

Tied Loan

A loan made by a government agency that requires a foreign borrower to spend the proceeds in the lender's country.

Tier 1 and Tier 2

Descriptions of the capital adequacy of banks. Tier 1 refers to core capital while Tier 2 refers to items such as undisclosed resources.

TIGER

Acronym for Treasury Investors Growth Receipt. US government-backed bonds without coupons, meaning that the bondholders do not receive the periodic interest payments. The principal of the bond and the individual coupons are sold separately.

Tight

In line with or extremely close to the inside market or last sale in a stock (+/- 1/8). On the money.

Tight market

A market in which volume is high, trading is active and highly competitive, and consequently spreads between bid and ask prices are narrow.

Tight money

When a restricted money supply makes credit difficult to secure. The antithesis of tight money is easy money.

Tiki

Tick of Dow Jones Industrial Average component issues.

Tilted portfolio

An indexing strategy that is linked to active management through the emphasis of a particular industry sector, selected performance factors such as earnings momentum, dividend yield, price-earnings ratio, or selected economic factors such as interest rates and inflation.

Time decay

Related: Theta.

Time deposit

Interest-bearing deposit at a savings institution that has a specific maturity. Related: Certificate of deposit.

Time Draft

A draft that matures either a certain number of days after acceptance or a certain number of days after the date of the draft. Compare Date draft and Sight draft

Time horizon

The period, usually expressed in years, for which an investor expects to hold an investment.

Time Letter of Credit

See: Usance Letter of Credit.

Timeliness

A source of competitive advantage that depends on

being the first to enter a given market with a product or service.

Time order

Order that becomes a market or limited price order or is canceled at a specific time.

Time premium

Also called time value, the amount by which an option price exceeds its intrinsic value. The value of an option beyond its current exercise value representing the optionholder's control until expiration, the risk of the underlying asset, and the riskless return.

Time-series analysis

Assessment of relationships between two or among more variables over periods of time.

Time series models

Systems that examine series of historical data; sometimes used as a means of technical forecasting, by examining moving averages.

Times-interest-earned ratio

Earnings before interest and tax, divided by interest payments.

Time spread strategy

Buying and selling puts and calls with the same exercise price but different expiration dates, and trying to profit from the different premiums of the options.

Time to maturity

The time remaining until a financial contract expires. Also called time until expiration.

Time until expiration

The time remaining until a financial contract expires. Also called time to maturity.

Time value

Applies to derivative products. Portion of an option price that is in excess of the intrinsic value, due to the amount of volatility in the stock; sometime referred to as premium. Time value is positively related to the length of time remaining until expiration.

Time value of money

The idea that a dollar today is worth more than a dollar in the future, because the dollar received today can earn interest up until the time the future dollar is received.

Time value of an option

The portion of an option's premium that is based on the amount of time remaining until the expiration date of the option contract, and the idea that the underlying components that determine the value of the option may change during that time. Time value is generally equal to the difference between the premium and the intrinsic value. Related: In the money.

Time value permium

The amount by which an option's total premium exceeds its intrinsic value.

Time-weighted rate of return

Related: Geometric mean return.

Timing

See: Market timing.

Timing option

The seller's choice of when in the delivery month to deliver. A Treasury Bond or note futures contract.

Tip

Information given by one trader to another, which is

used in making buy or sell decisions but is not available to the general public.

Tired

Has been strong for a while and will probably fall due to increased supply at current price level (due to e.g. profit taking, technical analysis). Heavy.

TITAL

See: Transaction insured trade acceptance locator.

Title insurance

Insurance policy that protects a policyholder from future challenges to the title claim a property that may result in loss of the property.

TJ

The two-character ISO 3166 country code for TAJIKISTAN.

TJR

The ISO 4217 currency code for the Tajikistan Rouble.

TK

The two-character ISO 3166 country code for TOKELAU.

TM

The two-character ISO 3166 country code for TURKMENISTAN.

TMM

The ISO 4217 currency code for the Turkmenistan Manet.

TN

The two-character ISO 3166 country code for TUNISIA.

TND

The ISO 4217 currency code for the Tunisian Dinar.

TO

The two-character ISO 3166 country code for TONGA.

To be announced (TBA)

A contract for the purchase or sale of an MBS to be delivered at an agreed-upon future date but does not include a specified pool number and number of pools or precise amount to be delivered.

Tobin's Q

Market value of assets divided by replacement value of assets. A Tobin's Q ratio greater than 1 indicates the firm has done well with its investment decisions. Named after James Tobin, Yale University economist.

Toehold purchase

Often used in risk arbitrage. Accumulation by an acquirer of less than 5% of the shares of a target company. Once 5% is acquired, the acquirer must file with the SEC and other agencies to explain its intentions and notify the acquiree. See: Rule 13d.

Tokyo Commodity Exchange (TOCOM)

Tokyo exchange for trading futures on gold, silver, platinum, palladium, rubber, cotton yarn, and woolen yarn.

Tokyo International Financial Futures Exchange

Exchange that trades Euroyen futures and options, and futures on the one-year Euroyen, three-month eurodollar, and US dollar/Japanese yen currency.

Tokyo Stock Exchange (TSE)

The largest stock exchange in Japan with the some of the most active trading in the world.

Toll revenue bond

A municipal bond that is repaid with revenues from tolls that are paid by users of the public project built with the bond revenue.

Tolling agreement

An agreement to put a specified amount of raw material per period through a particular processing facility. For example, an agreement to process a specified amount of alumina into aluminum at a particular aluminum plant.

Tom next

Means to "tomorrow next.". In the interbank market in Eurodollar deposits and the foreign exchange market, the value (delivery) date on a tom next transaction is the next business day.

Tombstone

Advertisement listing the underwriters of a security issue.

Ton

$100 million in bond trader's terms.

Tonnage

Gross Tonnage - Total internal carrying capacity of a vessel expressed in measurement tons (one measurement ton = 100 cu. ft.).

Too-big-too-fail

Government practices that protect large banking organizations from the normal discipline of the marketplace because of concerns that such institutions are so important to markets and their positions so intertwined with those of other banks that their failure would be unaccrptably disruptive, financially and economically.

TOP

The ISO 4217 currency code for the Tonga Pa'anga.

Top

Indicates the higher price one is willing to pay for a stock in an order; implies a not held order.

Top-down approach

A method of security selection that starts with asset allocation and works systematically through sector and industry allocation to individual security selection.

Top-down equity management style

Investment style that begins with an assessment of the overall economic environment and makes a general asset allocation decision regarding various sectors of the financial markets and various industries. The bottom-up manager, in contrast, selects specific securities within the particular sectors.

Top-heavy

At a price level where supply is exceeding demand. See: Resistance level.

Topline growth

Growth in revenues. Also see: Bottomline growth.

Topping out

Denoting a market or a security that is at the end of a period of rising prices and can now be expected to stay on a plateau or even to decline.

Toronto Stock Exchange (TSE)

Canada's largest stock exchange, trading approximately 1,200 company stocks and 33 options.

Total

Complete amount of buy or sell interest, as opposed to having more behind it. See: Partial.

Total asset turnover

The ratio of net sales to total assets.

Total capitalization

The total long-term debt and all types of equity of a company that constitutes its capital structure.

Total cost

The price paid for a security plus the broker's commission and any accrued interest that is owed to the seller (in the case of a bond).

Total debt-to-equity ratio

A capitalization ratio comparing current liabilities plus long-term debt to shareholders' equity.

Total dollar return

The dollar return on a nondollar investment, which includes the sum of any dividend/interest income, capital gains or losses, and currency gains or losses on the investment. See also: Total return.

Total Market Capitalization

The total market value of all of a firm's outstanding securities.

Total return

In performance measurement, the actual rate of return realized over some evaluation period. In fixed income analysis, the potential return that considers all three sources of return (coupon interest, interest on coupon interest, and any capital gain/loss) over some investment horizon.

Total return for calendar year

The profit or loss realized by an investment at the end of a specified calendar year, stated as the percentage gained or lost per dollar invested on January 1.

Total revenue

Total sales and other revenue for the period shown. Known as "turnover" in the U.K.

Total risk

The sum of systematic and unsystematic risk.

Total volume

The total number of shares or contracts traded on national and regional exchanges in a stock, bond, commodity, future, or option on a certain day.

Touch, the

Mainly applies to international equities. Inside market in London terminology.

Tough on price

Firm price mentality at which one wishes to transact stock, often at a discount/premium that is not available at the time.

Tout

To promote a security in order to attract buyers.

TP

The two-character ISO 3166 country code for EAST TIMOR.

T-period holding-period return

The percentage return over the T-year period an investment is held.

T+3

The settlement date for securities transactions such as a stock sale. It refers to the obligation in the brokerage business to settle securities trades by the third day following the trade date. The settlement occurs when the seller receives the sales price (the broker's commission) and the buyer receives the shares.

TR

The two-character ISO 3166 country code for TURKEY.

Tracking error

In an indexing strategy, the standard deviation of the difference between the performance of the benchmark and the replicating portfolio.

Tracking stock

Best defined with an example. Suppose Company A purchases a business from Company B and pays B with 1 million shares of A's stock. The agreement provides that B cannot sell the 1 million shares for 60 days, and also prohibits B from hedging by purchasing put options on A's shares or short-selling A's shares. B is worried that the market may fall in the next 60 days. B could hedge by purchasing put options or selling the futures on the S&P 500. However, it is possible that A's business is much more cyclical than the S&P 500. One solution to this problem is to find a tracking stock. This is a stock that has high correlation with A. Let us call it Company C. The solution is to sell short or buy protective put options on this tracking stock C. This protects B from fluctuations in the price of A's stock over the next 60 days. Because the degree of the protection is related to the correlation of A and C's stock, it is extremely unlikely that the protection is perfect.

Tracking stock is also used for internal evaluation. A firm with four divisions, for example, might set up four tracking stocks. The value-weighted sum of the four stocks exactly equals the firm's stock price observed in the market. This is a way to reward managers for good divisional performance with an equity that is tied to their division-rather than potentially penalizing them compensation for bad performance in a division they have no control over.

Trade

An oral (or electronic) transaction involving one party buying a security from another party. Once a trade is consummated, it is considered "done" or final. Settlement occurs 1-5 business days later.

Trade acceptance

Written demand that has been accepted by an industrial company to pay a given sum at a future date. Related: Banker's acceptance.

Trade Act of 1974

Legislation enacted late in 1974 and signed into law in January 1975, granting the President broad authority to enter into international agreements to reduce import barriers. Major purposes were to: (a) stimulate U.S. economic growth and to maintain and enlarge foreign markets for the products of U.S. agriculture, industry, mining and commerce; (b) strengthen economic relations with other countries through open and non-discriminatory trading practices; (c) protect American industry and workers against unfair or injurious import competition; and (d) provide "adjustment assistance" to industries, workers and communities injured or threatened by increased imports.

The Act allowed the President to extend tariff preferences to certain imports from developing countries and set conditions under which Most-Favored-Nation Treatment could be extended to non-market economy countries and provided negotiating authority for the Tokyo Round of multilateral trade negotiations.

Trade Adjustment Assistance

TAA for firms and workers is authorized by the 1974 Trade Act. TAA for firms is administered by Commerce; TAA for workers is administered by Labor.

Eligible firms must show that increased imports of articles like or directly competitive with those produced by the firm contributed importantly to declines in its sales and/or production and to the separation or threat of separation of a significant portion of the firm's workers. These firms receive help through Trade Adjustment Assistance Centers (TAACs), primarily in implementing adjustment strategies in production, marketing, and management.

Eligible workers must be associated with a firm whose sales or production have decreased absolutely due to increases in like or directly competitive imported products resulting in total or partial separation of the employee and the decline in the firm's sales or production. Assistance includes training, job search and relocation allowances, plus reemployment services for workers adversely affected by the increased imports.

Trade Adjustment Assistance Centers

TAACs are nonprofit, nongovernment organizations established to help firms qualify for and receive assistance in adjusting to import competition. TAACs are funded by the Commerce Department as a primary source of technical assistance to certified firms.

Trade Agreements Act of 1979

Legislation authorizing the U.S. to implement trade agreements dealing with non-tariff barriers negotiated during the Tokyo Round, including agreements that required changes in existing U.S. laws, and certain concessions that had not been explicitly authorized by the Trade Act of 1974. The Act incorporated into

U.S. law the Tokyo Round agreements on dumping, customs valuation, import licensing procedures, government procurement practices, product standards, civil aircraft, meat and dairy products, and liquor duties. The Act also extended the President's authority to negotiate trade agreements with foreign countries to reduce or eliminate non-tariff barriers to trade.

Trade and Development Agency

TDA grants funds for feasibility studies for large projects on the condition that U.S. firms are used to do the study. Should the project sponsor (usually a foreign government) agree to this condition, the opportunity to do the feasibility study generally is competed among all interested U.S. companies. The project sponsor chooses the company it wants to do the study and enters into a contractual relationship with that company, with TDA underwriting expenses.

Trade away

Trade execution by another broker/dealer.

Trade balance

Overall result of a country's exports.

Trade Barriers

The United States Trade Representative classifies trade barriers into eight general categories: (1) import policies (tariffs and other import charges, quantitative restrictions, import licensing, and customs barriers); (2) standards, testing, labeling, and certification; (3) government procurement; (4) export subsidies; (5) lack of intellectual property protection; (6) service barriers; (7) investment barriers; and (8) other barriers (e.g., barriers encompassing more than one category or barriers affecting a single sector).

Trade Concordance

Trade concordance refers to the matching of Harmonized System (HS) codes to larger statistical definitions, such as the Standard Industrial Classification (SIC) code and the Standard International Trade Classification (SITC) system. The Bureau of the Census, the United Nations, as well as individual Federal and private organizations, maintain trade concordances for the purpose of relating trade and production data.

Trade credit

Credit one firm grants to another firm for the purchase of goods or services.

Trade date

The date that the counterparties in an interest rate swap commit to the swap. Also, the day on which a security or a commodity future trade actually takes place. Trades generally settle (are paid for) 1-5 business days after a trade date. With stocks, settlement is generally 3 business days after the trade. The settlement date usually follows the trade date by five business days, but varies depending on the transaction and method of delivery used.

Trade debt

Accounts payable.

Trade deficit or surplus

The difference in the value of a nation's imports over exports (deficit) or exports over imports (surplus).

Trade Diversion

Trade diversion refers to the situation in which imports from free trade agreement member countries increase, displacing (or substituting) imports from nonmember countries.

Trade draft

A draft addressed to a commercial enterprise. See: Draft.

Trade Event

A trade event is a promotional activity that may include a demonstration of products or services and brings together in one viewing area the principals in the purchase and sale of the products or services. As a generic term, trade events may include trade fairs, trade missions, trade shows, catalog shows, matchmaker events, foreign buyer missions, and similar functions.

Trade Expansion Act of 1962

The Act provided authority for U.S. participation in the Kennedy Round of the GATT. The legislation granted the President general authority to negotiate, on a reciprocal basis, reductions of up to 50 percent in U.S. tariffs.

The Act explicitly eliminated the "Peril Point" provision that had limited U.S. negotiating positions in earlier GATT Rounds, and instead called on the Tariff Commission, the U.S. International Trade Commission, and other federal agencies to provide information regarding the probable economic effects of specific tariff concessions.

This Act superseded the Trade Agreements Act of 1934, as amended.

Trade Fair

A trade fair is a stage-setting event in which firms of several nationalities present their products or services to prospective customers in a pre-formatted setting (usually a booth of a certain size which is located adjacent to other potential suppliers). A distinguishing factor between trade fairs and trade shows is size. A trade fair is generally viewed as having a larger number of participants than other trade events, or as an event bringing together related industries.

Trade Fair Certification Program

The Commerce Department Trade Fair Certification program was started in 1983 to promote selected privately organized trade shows. The program helps private sector organizations in mounting certified international fairs. Commerce assistance includes promoting the fair among foreign customers and helping exhibitors to make commercial contacts.

Trade flat

For convertibles, trade without accrued interest. Preferred stock always "trades flat," as do bonds on which interest is in default or is in doubt. In general, trade in and out of a position at the same price, neither making a profit nor taking a loss.

Trade house

A firm that deals in actual commodities.

Trade Information Center

The Trade Information Center, TIC, is a one-stop source for information on Federal programs to assist U.S. exporters. Telephone: 1-800-USA-TRADE (1-800-872-8723).

Trade Lanes

The direction of trade, e.g. US to Europe.

Trademark

A distinctive name or symbol used to identify a product or company and build recognition. Trademarks may be registered with the US Patent and Trademark Office.

"Trade me out"

Work out of one's long position (usually created by committing firm principal to complete a trade block trade) by selling stock. Antithesis of "buy them back."

Trade Mission

Generically, a trade mission is composed of individuals who are taken as a group to meet with prospective customers overseas. Missions visit specific individuals or places with no specific stage setting other than appointments. Appointments are made with government and/or commercial customers, or with individuals who may be a stepping stone to customers.

ITA trade missions are scheduled in selected countries to help participants find local agents, representatives, and distributors, to make direct sales, or to conduct market assessments. Some missions include technical seminars to support sales of sophisticated products and technology in specific markets. ITA missions include planning and publicity, appointments with qualified contacts and with government officials, market briefings and background information on contacts, as well as logistical support and interpreter service. Trade missions also are frequently organized by other Federal, State, or local agencies.

Trade Negotiations Committee

The TNC is the steering group which manages the Uruguay Round negotiations. The TNC is comprised of all countries participating in the current negotiations (that is, it is not limited simply to members of the GATT). Functioning at the non-ministerial level, the TNC serves as a vehicle for transparency.

Trade on the wire

Immediately give a bid or offer to a salesperson without checking the floor conditions (listed), dealer depth

(OTC) or customer interest. An aggressive trading posture.

Trade on top of

Trade at a narrow speed or no spread in basis points relative to some other bond yield, usually Treasury bonds.

Trade Opportunities Program

The Trade Opportunities Program (TOP) is an International Trade Administration service which provides sales leads from overseas firms seeking to buy or represent U.S. products and services. Through overseas channels, U.S. foreign commercial officers gather leads and details, including specifications, quantities, end use, and delivery deadlines. TOPs are cabled to Washington and listed on the Commerce Department's Economic Bulletin Board and redistributed by the private sector.

Trade Policy Information System

The TPIS serves as a primary electronic repository of detailed current and historical trade data, including: (a) U.S. foreign trade data – the detailed U.S. merchandise trade statistics compiled by the Bureau of the Census, (b) United Nations trade data — trade statistics of over 170 reporting countries on a comparable basis, and (c) International Monetary Fund and World Bank databases — multi-country statistics on international finance, direction of trade, and developing country debt. TPIS provides a processing capabilities to: (a) obtain and disseminate trade data required for formulating and implementing U.S. trade policy and for export development, (b) provide analytical support to the Trade Promotion Coordinating Committee, and (c) meet the information needs of the U.S. Government trade community and the private sector.

Trade Policy Committee

The TPC is a cabinet-level, interagency trade committee established by the Trade Expansion Act of 1962 (chaired by the USTR) to provide broad guidance on trade issues. The Committee was renewed by an Executive Order at the end of the Carter Administration. Toward the end of the first Reagan administration, with much dissension over Japan policy between the TPC, the Senior Interagency Group (chaired by Treasury), and the other groups, the White House created the Economic Policy Council (EPC) in 1985 as a single forum to reduce tensions.

The Trade Policy Review Group (TPRG)

Is a subcabinet group which meets about once a week. The TPRG is an ad hoc creation that was not established by law. TPRG membership is fairly fluid; so that agencies which want to participate in a particular discussion can sit at the table.

The Trade Policy Staff Committee (TPSC)

Has met perhaps once a year since 1988. TPSC was established by law to obtain advice from the private sector on topics such as retaliation; it generally serves as a paper clearance structure.

Beneath the TPSC is a large number (60-to-100, exact counts are not maintained) of TPSC subcommittees. Subcommittees are not independent; they are established ad referendum, to deal with topics of interim interest and are sometimes no more than phone and fax lists of interested parties on a given issue.

Trade Policy Review Mechanism

The TPRM was created at the Uruguay Round mid-term ministerial meeting in Montreal. Under the TPRM, the trade policies of any GATT contracting party are subject to regularly scheduled review by the

GATT Council. Reviews may lead to recommendations on ways to improve a contracting party's trade policies.

Trade Promotion Coordinating Committee

The TPCC provides a means for all Federal agencies to coordinate their trade promotion activities, eliminate duplication, and to provide a more focused U.S. Government approach to trade promotion. Committee members include 19 Federal agencies: the Departments of Commerce (as chair), Agriculture, Defense, Energy, Interior, Labor, State, Transportation, and Treasury, the Agency for International Development, the Council of Economic Advisers, the Environmental Protection Agency, Eximbank, the Office of Management and Budget, the Overseas Private Investment Corporation, the Small Business Administration, the Trade and Development Agency, the U.S. Information Agency, and the U.S. Trade Representative. The TPCC formed working groups to aid in coordinating trade promotion programs. Thirteen working groups were operating at the end of 1992: (1) Trade Finance, (2) Food Production, Machinery and Processing, (3) Energy, Environment and Infrastructure, (4) Technology and Aerospace, (5) Services, (6) Enterprise for the Americas, (7) Eastern Europe, (8) Asia and Pacific, (9) State and Local, (10) Minority Business, (11) U.S. Asia Environmental Partnership, (12) Russia, Ukraine, and the Newly Independent States, and (13) Small Business. The TPCC was originally established by Executive Order of the President in May 1990. The Export Enhancement Act of (October) 1992 codified the TPCC. See: Advocacy Center Export Enhancement Act of 1992.

Trade-Related Aspects of Intellectual Property Rights

TRIPs refers to U.S. intellectual property rights objectives in the Uruguay Round. These objectives include achieving a comprehensive GATT agreement that would include: (a) substantive standards of protection for all areas of intellectual property (patents, trademarks, copyrights, etc.); (b) effective enforcement measures (both at the border and internally); and (c) effective dispute settlement provisions.

Trade-Related Investment Measures

TRIMs require the use of specified amounts of local inputs rather than imported goods, and requirements to export a certain amount of production. The developed countries (with the exception of Australia) favor prohibiting certain TRIMs; virtually all developing countries oppose prohibiting any TRIMs.

Trade reporting

Dealer: In a trade between two registered Market Participants (MP), only the sell side reports the trade. Auction: In a trade between two member firms, only the sell side reports the trade. Dealer: In a trade between a registered MP and a non-registered MP (Market Maker not registered in a particular stock, an ECN, etc.), the registered MP reports the trade as a buy or sell. Auction: Trading can occur ONLY between two member firms. (Thus, a buy is never reported.)

Traders

Individuals who take positions in securities and their derivatives with the objective of making profits. Traders can make markets by trading the flow. When they do this, their objective is to earn the bid/ask spread. Traders can also take proprietary positions in which they seek to profit from the directional movement of prices or spread positions.

Trades by appointment

A stock that is very difficult to trade to because of illiquidity.

Trade Show

A trade show is a stage-setting event in which firms present their products or services to prospective customers in a pre-formatted setting (usually a booth of a certain size which is located adjacent to other potential suppliers). The firms are generally in the same industry but not necessarily of the same nationality. A distinguishing factor between trade fairs and trade shows is size. A trade show is generally viewed as a smaller assembly of participants.

Trade Surplus

A nation's excess of exports over imports during a given time frame.

Trade-weight value of the dollar

The value of the dollar pegged to, a market basket of selected foreign currencies. The Federal Reserve calculates a trade-weighted value of the dollar based on the weighted-average exchange value of the dollar against the currencies of 10 industrial countries.

Trade with Foreign Countries

Puerto Rico is a Customs district within the U.S. Customs territory, and its trade with foreign countries is included in the U.S. export and import statistics. The U.S. export and import statistics include merchandise trade between the U.S. Virgin Islands and foreign countries even though the Virgin Islands of the United States are not officially a part of the U.S. Customs territory. Data on trade of other U.S. outlying possessions with foreign countries is not compiled by the United States.

Trading

Buying and selling securities.

Trading authorization

A document (power of attorney) a customer gives to a broker in order that the broker may buy and sell securities on behalf of the customer.

Trading costs

Costs of buying and selling marketable securities and borrowing. Trading costs include commissions, slippage, and the bid/ask spread. See: Transactions costs.

Trading desk (dealing desk)

Personnel at an international bank who trade spot and forward foreign exchange.

Trading dividends

Maximizing a firm's revenues by purchasing stock in other firms in order to collect the maximum amount of dividends of which 70% is tax-free.

Trading halt

When trading of a stock, bond, option or futures contract is stopped by an exchange while news is being broadcast about the security. See: Suspended trading.

Trading limit

The exchange-imposed maximum daliy price change that a futures contract or futures option contract can undergo.

Trading paper

CDs purchased by accounts that are likely to resell them. The term is commonly used in the Euromarket.

Trading pattern

Long-range direction of a security or commodity futures price, charted by drawing one line connecting the highest prices the security has reached and another line connecting the lowest prices at which the security has traded over the same period. See: Technical analysis.

Trading posts

The positions on the floor of a stock exchange where the specialists stand and securities are traded.

Trading price

The price at which a security is currently selling.

Trading profit

The profit earned on short-term trades of securities held for less than one year, subject to tax at normal income tax rates.

Trading range

The difference between the high and low prices traded during a period of time; for commodities, the high/low price limit an exchange establishes for a specific commodity for any one day's trading.

Trading symbol

See: Ticker symbol

Trading unit

The number of shares of a particular security that is used as the acceptable quantity for trading on the exchanges.

Trading variation

The increments to which securities prices are rounded up or rounded down.

Trading volume

The number of shares transacted every day. As there is a seller for every buyer, one can think of the trading volume as half of the number of shares transacted.

That is, if A sells 100 shares to B, the volume is 100 shares.

Traditional IRA

A tax-deferred individual retirement account that allows annual contributions of up to $2000 for each income earner. Contributions are fully deductible for all individuals who are not active participants in employer-sponsored plans or for plan participants within certain income ranges.

Traditional view (of dividend policy)

An argument that, "within reason," investors prefer higher dividends to lower dividends because the dividend is sure but future capital gains are uncertain.

Trailing earnings

Past earnings. Often used in the context of the price earnings ratio. This ratio is usually distinguished as price to trailing earnings (today's price divided by the most recent 12 months of earnings) versus price to prospective earnings (today's price divided by consensus forecast earnings for the next 12 months).

Trailing sales

Past sales. Often used in the valuation of companies that have negative cash flows or earnings. The company is said to be valued at some multiple of past sales - usually, the last 12 months sales.

Tramp Steamer

A ship not operating on regular routes or schedules.

Tranche

One of several related securities offered at the same time. Tranches from the same offering usually have different risk, reward, and/or maturity characteristics.

Transaction

The delivery of a security by a seller and its acceptance by the buyer.

Transaction account

A checking or similar account from which transfers can be made to third parties. Demand-deposit accounts, negotiable order of withdrawal NOW accounts, automatic transfer service (ATS) accounts, and credit union share draft accounts are examples of transaction accounts at banks and other depository institutions.

Transaction demand (for money)

The money needed to accommodate a firm's expected cash transactions.

Transaction exposure

Risk to a firm with known future cash flows in a foreign currency, that arises from possible changes in the exchange rate. Related: Translation exposure.

Transaction fee

A charge an intermediary, such as a broker-dealer or a bank, assesses for assisting in the sale or purchase of a security.

Transaction Insured Trade Acceptance Locator (TITAL)

A trade acceptance through an insurance entity (rather than a bank) which is conditional upon exporter performance.

Transaction loan

A loan extended by a bank for a specific purpose. Lines of credit and revolving credit agreements involve by contrast loans that can be used for various purposes.

Transactions costs

The time, effort, and money necessary, including such things as commission fees and the cost of physically moving the asset from seller to buyer. Transactions costs should also include the bid/ask spread as well as price impact costs (for example a large sell order could lower the price). Related: Round-trip transactions costs, information costs, search costs.

Transactions motive

A desire to hold cash in order to conduct cash-based transactions.

Transaction Statement

A document that delineates the terms and conditions agreed upon between the importer and exporter.

Transaction tax

Applies mainly to international equities. Levies on a deal that foreign governments sometimes charge.

Transaction Risk

The risk of changes in the home currency value of a specific future foreign currency cash flow.

Transcript of Account

A listing of all prior and present registered securityholder account information.

Transfer

A change of ownership from one person or party to another.

Transfer agent

Individual or institution a company appoints to look after the transfer of securities.

Transfer On Death (TOD)

The process of changing title of a security from one name to another upon the death of one of the title-holders.

Transfer payments

Payments from a government to its citizens, such as welfare and other government benefits.

Transfer price

The price at which one unit of a firm sells goods or services to another unit of the same firm.

Transfer tax

A small federal tax on the movement of ownership of all bonds (except obligations of the US, foreign governments, states, and municipalities) and all stocks.

Transferable letter of credit

Document that allows the first beneficiary on a standby bank assurance of funds to transfer all or part of the original letter of credit to a third party.

Transferable Stock Options

Options that provide by their terms that they may be transferred by the optionee, generally only to a family member or to a trust, limited partnership or other entity for the benefit of family members, or to a charity.

Transferable put right

An option issued by a firm to its shareholders to sell the firm one share of its common stock at a fixed price (the strike price) within a stated period (the time to maturity). The put right is "transferable" because it can be traded in the capital markets.

Transferee

The party who has received the benefits of a letter of credit by action of a transfer.

Transferor

The beneficiary of a transferable letter of credit who causes a bank to transfer the credit to another party.

Transition phase

A stage of development when a company begins to mature and its earnings decelerate to the rate of growth of the economy as a whole. Related: Three-phase DDM.

Transit Shipment

A term designating a shipment destined for an interior point or a place best reached by reshipment from another port.

Transit Zones

Transit zones, a form of free trade zone, are ports of entry in coastal countries that are established as storage and distribution centers for the convenience of a neighboring country lacking adequate port facilities or access to the sea. A transit zone is administered so that goods in transit to and from the neighboring country are not subject to the customs duties, import controls or many of the entry and exit formalities of the host country. Transit zones are more limited facilities then a foreign trade zone or a free port. See: Free Trade Zones.

Translation exposure

Risk of adverse effects on a firm's financial statements that may arise from changes in exchange rates. Related: Transaction exposure.

Translation Risk

The risk of changes in the reported home currency accounting results of foreign operations due to changes in currency exchange rates.

Transmittal Letter

A list of the particulars of the shipment and a record of the documents being transmitted together with instructions for disposition of documents. Any special instructions are also included.

Transnational Corporation

A TNC is a company which operates in a home country and has an affiliate overseas. The terms transnational corporation and multinational corporation are now used synonymously. Through the 1970s and 1980's the United Nations attempted to assess the impact of TNCs on development and international relations in the world economy. These efforts resulted in considerable complexity in attempting to define a TNC, including associations with impact on developing countries, size, ownership, and other characteristics. Agreement on a specialized definition was never achieved.

Transparency

The extent to which laws, regulations, agreements, and practices affecting international trade are open, clear, measurable, and verifiable.

Transshipment

Transshipment refers to the act of sending an exported product through an intermediate country before routing it to the country intended to be its final destination. See: Pass-through.

Travel Advisory Program

The Department of State manages a travel advisory program which publicizes travel warnings and consular information. Both travel warnings and consular information sheets are available through the Citizens' Emergency Center's automated answering system: 202-647-5225.

Travel and entertainment expense

Funds spent on business travel and entertainment that qualify for a tax deduction of 50% of the amount claimed.

Travel Mission

A travel mission is a marketing activity carried out in foreign markets which usually involves trade information, presentations, and media activities.

Travel Warning

See: Travel Advisory Program.

Treasurer

The corporate officer responsible for designing and implementing a firm's financing and investing activities.

Treasurer's check

A check issued by a bank to make a payment. Treasurer's checks outstanding are counted as part of a bank's reservable deposits and as part of the money supply.

Treasuries

Related: Treasury securities.

Treasury

US Department of the Treasury, which issues all Treasury bonds, notes, and bills as well as overseeing agencies. Also, the department within a corporation that oversees its financial operations including the issuance of new shares.

Treasury bills

Debt obligations of the US Treasury that have maturities of one year or less. Maturities for T-bills are usually 91 days, 182 days, or 52 weeks.

Treasury bonds

Debt obligations of the US Treasury that have maturities of 10 years or more.

Treasury direct

A system allowing an individual investor to make a noncompetitive bid on US Treasury securities and thus avoid broker-dealer fees.

Treasury notes

Debt obligations of the US Treasury that have maturities of more than 2 years but less than 10 years.

Treasury securities

Securities issued by the US Department of the Treasury.

Treasury Shares

Shares issued in the name of the Corporation. The shares are considered issued, but not outstanding.Usually refers to stock that was once traded in the market but has since been repurchased by the corporation. Treasury stock not considered when calculating dividends or earnings per share.

Treasury stock

Common stock that has been repurchased by the company and held in the company's treasury.

Treaties and Other International Acts Series

When a treaty or an executive agreement is first published by the United States, it is assigned a TIAS number and published in slip form in the Treaties and other

International Acts Series. TIAS, published by the Department of State, is a series of individual pamphlets.

Treaties in Force

Treaties In Force, published annually by the Department of State, lists all treaties and executive agreements, both bilateral and multilateral, which are considered to be in force for the United States as of January 1 of the respective year.

" Treat me subject "

In the equities market, a conditional bid or offer. "My bid or offer is not firm, but is subject to confirmation between other parties and to market changes."

Treaty

See: Interntional Agreements.

Treaty of European Union

See: Maastricht Treaty.

Treaty of Rome

The Treaty of Rome, enacted in March 1957, established a European customs union and required the elimination of all quantitative restrictions and other measures having an equivalent effect on trade among the European signatory member states. It was intended to create a single market with free movement of goods, persons, services, and capital and envisioned a single internal European market. It became the founding charter for the European Economic Community, which came into being on January 1, 1958. The Treaty had no provisions for monetary arrangements. Accomplishments following the treaty included completion of the customs union and establishment of the Common Agricultural Policy (CAP). See: Maastricht Treaty.

Trend

The general direction of the market.

Trend Ratio Analysis

The comparison of the successive values of each ratio for a single firm over a number of years.

Trendline

A technical chart line that depicts the past movement of a security and that is used in an attempt to help predict future price movements.

Treynor Index

A measure of the excess return per unit of risk, where excess return is defined as the difference between the portfolio's return and the risk-free rate of return over the same evaluation period and where the unit of risk is the portfolio's beta. Named after Jack Treynor.

T-Rex Fund

A large venture capital fund (over one billion dollars). Such funds are known for imposing strong discipline on the firms they fund.

Triangular arbitrage

Striking offsetting deals among three markets simultaneously to obtain an arbitrage profit.

Trickle down

An economic theory that the support of businesses that allows them to flourish will eventually benefit middle- and lower-income people, in the form of increased economic activity and reduced unemployment.

Trigger Price Mechanism

The TPM is an antidumping mechanism designed to protect U.S. industries from underpriced imports. First used in 1978 to protect the steel industry, the TPM is the price of the lowest cost foreign producer. Imports priced below the trigger price are assessed a duty equal to the difference between their price and the trigger price.

TRIN

Name derived from TRading INdex. Also known as an ARMS index. The index is usually calculated as the number of advancing issues divided by the number of declining issues. This, in turn, is divided by the advancing volume divided by the declining volume. If there is considerably more advancing volume relative to declining volume this will tend to reduce the index (i.e. increase the denominator). Hence, a value less than 1.0 is bullish while values greater than 1.0 indicate bearish demand. The index often is smoothed with a simple moving average.

Triple net lease

A lease providing that the tenant pay for all maintenance expenses, plus utilities, taxes, and insurance. This results in lower risk for investors, who usually form a limited partnership.

Triple tax-exempt

Municipal bonds featuring federal, state, and local tax-free interest payments.

Triple witching hour

The four times a year that the S&P futures contract expires at the same time as the S&P 100 index option contract and option contracts on individual stocks. It is the last trading hour on the third Friday of March, June, September, and December, when stock options, futures on stock indexes, and options on these futures expire concurrently. Massive trades in index futures, options, and underlying stock by hedge strategists and arbitrageurs cause abnormal activity (noise) and volatility.

TRL

The ISO 4217 currency code for the Turkish Lira.

Tropical Products

Traditionally, agricultural goods of export interest to developing countries in the tropical zones of Africa, Latin America, and East Asia (coffee, tea, spices, bananas, and tropical hardwoods).

Trough

The transition point between economic recession and recovery.

Truck Bill of Lading (Waybill or Pro)

A non-negotiable bill of lading for domestic transport. The bill is issued in one original only if it evidences a contract for delivery of the goods (in either "long form" or "short form"), a receipt for the goods, and title to the goods, but no rates or freight charges are shown. However, any party may sign at destination on behalf of the consignee unless "signature service' is required by the shipper, in which case only the party named as consignee may endorse the bill of lading. In addition, insurance may be offered as in air waybills.

True interest cost

For a security such as commercial paper that is sold on a discount basis, true interest cost is the coupon rate required to provide an identical return assuming a coupon-bearing instrument of like maturity that pays interest in arrears.

True lease

A contract that qualifies as a valid lease agreement under the Internal Revenue Code.

Trust

A fiduciary relationship calling for a trustee to hold the title to assets for the benefit of the beneficiary. The person creating the trust, who may or may not also be the beneficiary, is called the grantor.

Trust company

An organization that acts as a fiduciary and administers trusts.

Trust deed

Agreement between trustee and borrower setting out terms of a bond.

Trustee

Agent of a bond issuer who handles the administrative aspects of a loan and ensures that the borrower complies with the terms of the bond indenture.

Trustee in bankruptcy

An appointed trustee who supervises and administers the affairs of a bankrupt company or individual.

Trust fund transaction

An intra budgetary financial arrangement in which both payments and receipts occur within the same trust fund group.

Trust Indenture Act of 1939

A law that requires all corporate bonds and other debt securities to be issued subject to indenture agreements and comply with certain indenture provisions approved by the SEC.

Trust Receipt

An undertaking signed by a buyer, against which a bank releases merchandise for the purpose of manufacture or sale, but retains title thereto. The buyer assumes the obligation of maintaining the identity of the merchandise, or the processing thereof, distinct from other assets and to hold them subject to repossession by the bank.

Truth in lending law

Legislation governing the granting of credit, that requires lenders to disclose the true cost of loans and the actual interest rates and terms of the loans in a manner that is easily understood.

TSE 300 (Toronto Stock Exchange 100 index)

Canadian form of a S&P 500.

TT

The two-character ISO 3166 country code for TRINIDAD AND TOBAGO.

TT&L account

Treasury tax and loan account at a bank.

TTD

The ISO 4217 currency code for the Trinidad and Tobago Dollar.

TTM

Trailing 12 months. Often used with Earnings Per Share.

Turkey

A losing investment.

Turn

In the equities market, a reversal; unwind.

Turnaround

Securities bought and sold for settlement on the same day. Also describes a firm that has been performing poorly, but changes its financial course and improves its performance.

Turnaround time

Time available or needed to effect a turnaround.

Turnkey

A method of construction whereby the contractor assumes total responsibility from design through completion of the project.

Turnkey construction contract

A type of construction contract under which the construction firm is obligated to complete a project according to prespecified criteria for a price that is fixed at the time the contract is signed.

Turnover

For mutual funds, a measure of trading activity during the previous year, expressed as a percentage of the average total assets of the fund. A turnover rate of 25% means that the value of trades represented one-fourth of the assets of the fund. For finance, the number of times a given asset, such as inventory, is replaced during the accounting period, usually a year. For corporate finance, the ratio of annual sales to net worth, representing the extent to which a company can grow without outside capital. For markets, the volume of shares traded as a percent of total shares listed during a specified period, usually a day or a year. For Great Britain, total revenue. Percentage of the total number of shares outstanding of an issue that trades during any given period.

Turnover rate

Measures trading activity during a particular period. Portfolios with high turnover rates incur higher transaction costs and are more likely to distribute capital gains, which are taxable to nonretirement accounts.

TV

The two-character ISO 3166 country code for TUVALU.

TW

The two-character ISO 3166 country code for TAIWAN, PROVINCE OF CHINA.

TWD

The ISO 4217 currency code for the Taiwan Dollar.

12B-1 fees

The percent of a mutual fund's assets used to defray marketing and distribution expenses. The amount of the fee is stated in the fund's prospectus. The SEC has recently proposed that 12B-1 fees in excess of 0.25% be classed as a load. A true no load fund has neither a sales charge nor a 12b-1 fee.

12B-1 funds

Mutual funds that do not charge an up-front or back-end commission, but instead take out up to 1.25% of average daily fund assets each year to cover the costs of selling and marketing shares, an arrangement allowed by the SEC's Rule 12B-1 (passed in 1980).

Twenty bond index

A benchmark indicator of the level of municipal bond yields. It consists of the yields on 20 general obligation municipal bonds with 20-year maturities with an average rating equivalent to a1l.

Twenty-day period

The period during which the SEC inspects registration statement and preliminary prospectus prior to a new issue or secondary distribution.

Twenty-Foot Equivalent Unit

TEU is a measure of a ship's cargo-carrying capacity. One TEU measures twenty feet by eight feet by eight feet — the dimensions of a standard twenty-foot container. An FEU (forty-foot equivalent unit) equals two TEUs.

20% cushion rule

Guideline that revenues from facilities financed by municipal bonds should exceed the operating budget plus maintenance costs and debt service by at least 20% to allow for unforeseen expenses.

25% rule

The guidelines that bonded debt over 25% of a municipality's annual budget is excessive.

Twisting

Convincing a customer that trades are necessary in order to generate a commission. This is an unethical practice.

Two dollar broker

Floor broker of the NYSE, who executes orders for other brokers having more business at that time than they can handle with their own private floor brokers or who do not have their exchange member on the floor.

Two-factor model

Usually, Fischer Black's zero-beta version of the capital asset pricing model. It may also refer to another type of model whereby expected returns are generated by any two factors.

Two-fund separation theorem

The theoretical result that all investors will hold a combination of the risk-free asset and the market portfolio.

Two-sided market

A market in which both bid and asked prices, good for the standard unit of trading, are quoted. When customers or market makers are lined up on both sides (buy and sell) of a stock.

Two-state option pricing model

A pricing equation allowing an underlying asset to assume only two possible (discrete) values in the next time period for each value it can take on in the preceding time period. Also called the binomial option pricing model.

Two-tier bid

Takeover bid in which the acquirer offers to pay more for the shares needed to gain control than for the remaining shares, or to pay the same price but at different times in the merger period; contrasts with any-or-all bid.

Two-tier tax system

Taxation system that results in taxing the income going to shareholders twice.

Type

The classification of an option contract as either a put or a call.

TZ

The two-character ISO 3166 country code for TANZANIA, UNITED REPUBLIC OF.

TZS

The ISO 4217 currency code for the Tanzania Shilling.

U

UA

The two-character ISO 3166 country code for UKRAINE.

UAH

The ISO 4217 currency code for the Ukraine Hryvnia.

UG

The two-character ISO 3166 country code for UGANDA.

UGX

The ISO 4217 currency code for the Uganda Shilling.

Ultimate Beneficial Owner

The UBO of a U.S. affiliate is that person, proceeding up the affiliate's ownership chain beginning with and including the foreign parent, that is not owned more than 50 percent by another person. The UBO consists of only the ultimate owner, other affiliated persons are excluded. If the foreign parènt is not owned more than 50 percent by another person, the foreign parent and the UBO are the same. A UBO, unlike a foreign parent, may be a U.S. person.

Ultimate Consignee

The ultimate consignee is the person located abroad who is the true party in interest, receiving the export for the designated end-use.

Ultra vires activities

Corporate actions and operations that are not sanctioned by corporate charter, sometimes leading to shareholder lawsuits.

Ultradot

Applies to derivative products. Firm proprietary software that stores, and sends baskets of stock through SEAQ to either the NYSE or the curb for program trading.

Ultra-short-term bond fund

A mutual fund that invests in bonds with very short maturity periods, usually one year or less.

UM

The two-character ISO 3166 country code for UNITED STATES MINOR OUTLYING ISLANDS.

Umbrella Agreements

As used in this publication, bilateral trade agreement between public agencies of two countries or a public agency and a foreign private enterprise. Umbrella agreements stipulate conditions for substantial trade turnovers, are reviewed on an annual basis, and provide for the inclusion of multiple trading parties.

Umbrella personal liability policy

A liability insurance policy that provides protection against damages not covered by standard liability policies, such as large jury awards in lawsuits.

Umbrella policy

Insurance for exports of an exporter whose issuer handles all administrative requirements.

Unamortized bond discount

Par value of a bond less the proceeds received from the sale of the bond, less whatever portion has been amortized.

Unamortized premiums on investments

The unexpensed portion of the difference between the price paid for a security and its par value.

Unbiased expectations hypothesis

Theory that forward exchange rates are unbiased predictors of future spot rates. See Forward parity.

Unbiased predictor

A theory that spot prices at some future date will be equal to today's forward rates.

Unbundling

Separation of a multinational firm's transfers of funds into discrete flows for specific purposes. See: Bundling.

Uncollected funds

The amount of bank deposits in the form of checks that have not yet been paid by the banks on which the checks are drawn.

Uncollectible account

An account which cannot be collected by a company because the customer is not able to pay or is unwilling to pay.

Unconfirmed Letter of Credit

A letter of credit which has not been guaranteed or confirmed by any bank other than the bank that opened it. The advising bank merely informs the beneficiary of the letter of credit terms and conditions.

Uncovered call

A short call option position in which the writer does not own shares of underlying stock represented by the option contracts. Uncovered calls are much riskier for the writer than a covered call, where the writer of the uncovered call owns the underlying stock. If the buyer of a call exercises the option to call, the writer would be forced to buy the asset at the current market price. Also called a "naked" asset.

Uncovered call writing

A short call option position in which the writer does not own an equivalent position in the underlying security represented by his option contracts.

Uncovered options

See: Naked options.

Uncovered put

A short put option position in which the writer does not have a corresponding short stock position or has not deposited, in a cash account, cash or cash equivalents equal to the exercise value of the put. The writer has pledged to buy the asset at a certain price if the buyer of the option chooses to exercise it. Uncovered put options limit the writer's risk to the value of the stock (adjusted for premium received.) Also called "naked" puts.

Uncovered Put writing

A short put option position in which the writer does not have a corresponding short position in the underlying security or has not deposited, in a cash account,

Under the belt

Long position in a stock.

Underbanked

When an originating investment banker cannot find enough firms to underwrite a new issue.

Underbooked

Describes limited interest by prospective buyers in a new issue of a security during the preoffering registration period.

Undercapitalized

A business has insufficient capital to carry out its normal functions.

Underfunded pension plan

A pension plan that has a negative surplus (i.e., liabilities exceed assets).

Underinvestment problem

The mirror image of the asset substitution problem, in that stockholders refuse to invest in low-risk assets to avoid shifting wealth from themselves to debtholders.

Underlying

What supports the security or instrument that parties agree to exchange in a derivative contract.

Underlying asset

The security or property or loan agreement that an option gives the option holder the right to buy or to sell.

Underlying debt

Municipal bonds issued by government entities but under the control of larger government entities and for which the larger entity shares the credit responsibility.

Underlying futures contract

A futures contract that supports an option on that future, which is executed if the option is exercised .

Underlying security

For options, the security that is subject to purchase or sold upon exercise of an option contract. For example, IBM stock is the underlying security for IBM options. For Depository receipts, the class, series, and number of the foreign shares represented by the depository receipt.

Undermargined account

A margin account that no longer meets minimum maintenance requirements, requiring a margin call on the investor.

Underperform

When a security is expected to, or does, appreciate at a slower rate than the overall market rate of performance.

Underpricing

Issuing securities at less than their market value.

Undervalued

A stock price perceived to be too low or cheap, as indicated by a particular valuation model. For instance, some might consider a particular company's stock price cheap if the company's price-earnings ratio is much lower than the industry average. To refer to undervaluation or overvaluation implicitly assumes some model of valuation. It is always possible that the security is valued correctly and that model applied is wrong.

Undervalued security

A security selling below its market value or liquidation value.

Underweight

Usually refers to recommendation that leads an investor to reduce their investment in a particular security or asset class. The reduction is usually with respect to a benchmark. Suppose that U.S. equities compose 40% of the benchmark portfolio. If one thinks the U.S. will underperform, the investor may reduce the exposure to U.S. equity to less than 40%.

Underwithholding

When a taxpayer has withheld too little tax from salary and will therefore owe tax when filing a return.

Underwrite

To guarantee, as to guarantee the issuer of securities a specified price by entering into a purchase and sale agreement. To bring securities to market.

Underwriter

A firm, usually an investment bank, that buys an issue of securities from a company and resells it to investors. In general, A party that guarantees the proceeds to the firm from a security sale, thereby in effect taking ownership of the securities.

Underwriter's discount

See: Gross spread.

Underwriting

Acting as the underwriter in the issue of new securities for a firm.

Underwriting agreement

The contract between a corporation issuing new publicly offered securities and the managing underwriter as agent for the underwriting group. Compare to agreement among underwriters.

Underwriting Commission

The fee investment bankers charge for underwriting a security issue.

Underwriting fee

The portion of the gross underwriting spread that compensates the securities firms that underwrite a public offering for their services.

Underwriting income

For an insurance company, the difference between the premiums earned and the costs of settling claims.

Underwriting spread

The income that is generated by the underwriting syndicate and the selling group, which is essentially the difference between the amount paid to the issuer of securities in a primary distribution and the public offering price.

Underwriting syndicate

A group of investment banks that work together to sell new security offerings to investors. The underwriting syndicate is led by the lead underwriter. See also: Lead underwriter.

Underwritten offering

A purchase and sale.

Undigested securities

Newly issued securities that are not purchased because of lack of demand during the initial public offering.

Undiversifiable risk

Related: Systematic risk.

Unearned income (revenue)

Income received in advance of the time at which it is earned, such as prepaid rent.

Unearned interest

Interest that has been received on a loan, but that cannot be treated as a part of earnings yet, because the principal of the loan has not been outstanding long enough.

Unemployment rate

The percentage of the people classified as unemployed as compared to the total labor force.

Unencumbered

Property that is not subject to any claims by creditors. For example, securities bought with cash instead of on margin and homes with mortgages paid off.

Unequal Voting

These provisions limit the voting rights of some shareholders and expand those of others. Under time-phased voting, shareholders who have held the stock for a given period of time are given more votes per share than recent purchases. Another variety is the substantial shareholder provision, which limits the voting power of shareholders who have exceeded a certain threshold of ownership.

Unfair Trade Practice

This term refers to any act, policy, or practice of a foreign government that: (a) violates, is inconsistent with, or otherwise denies benefits to the U.S. under any trade agreement to which the United States is a party; (b) is unjustifiable, unreasonable, or discriminatory and burdens or restricts United States commerce; or (c) is otherwise inconsistent with a favorable section 301 determination by the U.S. Trade Representative.

Unfavorable Balance of Trade

The value of a nation's imports in excess of the value of its exports.

Unfunded debt

Debt maturing within one year (short-term debt). See: Funded debt.

Unfunded pension plan

Provides for the employer to pay out amounts to retirees or beneficiaries as and when they are needed. There is no money put aside on a regular basis. Instead, it is taken out of current income.

Unified tax credit

A federal tax credit that reduces tax liability, dollar for dollar, on lifetime gifts and asset transfers at death.

Uniform Commercial Code (UCC)

Collection of laws dealing with commercial business.

Uniform Customs and Practices (Brochure 500)

International Chamber of Commerce rules (commonly referred to as UCP 500 or ICC 500), that are used for Letters of credit. These letters then become legally binding when written into the text of the letter.

Uniform Gifts to Minors Act (UGMA)

Legislation that provides a tax-effective manner of transferring property to minors without the complications of trusts or guardianship restrictions.

Uniform practice code

Standards of the NASD prescribing procedures for handling over-the-counter securities transactions, such as delivery, settlement date, and ex-dividend date.

Uniform Rules for Collections

International Chamber of Commerce rules on the handling of documentary and clean collections.

Uniform securities agent state law examination

A test required in some states for registered representatives who are employees of member firms of the NASD or over-the-counter brokers.

Uniform Transfers to Minors Act (UTMA)

A law similar to the Uniform Gifts to Minors Act that extends the definition of gifts to include real estate, paintings, royalties, and patents.

Unilateral transfers

Items in the current account of the balance of payments of a country's accounting books that correspond to gifts from foreigners or pension payments to foreign residents who once worked in the particular country.

Uninsured motorist insurance

Insurance that covers the policyholder and family if they are injured by a hit-and-run or uninsured motorist, assuming the other driver is at fault.

Union de Paises Exportadores de Banano

See: Union of Banana Exporting Countries.

Union Douanière et Economique de l'Afrique Centrale

See: Central African Customs and Economic Union.

Union du Maghreb Arabe

See: Arab Maghreb Union.

Union Internationale des Télécommunications

See: International Telecommunication Union.

Union Monétaire Quest-Africaine

See: West African Monetary Union.

Union of Banana Exporting Countries

The Union (Spanish: Union de Paises Exportadores de Banano, UPEB) promotes the banana industry among membes. The Union was established in 1974; headquarters are in Panama. Members include: Colombia, Costa Rica, Dominican Republic, Guatemala, Honduras, Nicaragua, Panaman, and Venezuela.

Unique Diversification Benefit

Reduction in the likelihood of financial distress for a conglomerate firm that comes with its diversified investments.

Unique risk

Also called unsystematic risk or idiosyncratic risk. Specific company risk that can be eliminated through diversification. See: Diversifiable risk and unsystematic risk.

Unissued stock

Shares authorized in a corporation's charter, but not issued.

Unit

More than one class of securities traded together (e.g., one common share and three subscription warrants).

Unit benefit formula

Method used to determine a participant's benefits in a defined benefit plan. Involves multiplying years of service by the percentage of salary.

United Nations

The UN is an international organization which was established in 1945 to: (a) maintain international peace and security; (b) develop friendly relations among nations, (c) achieve international cooperation in solving economic, social, cultural, and humanitarian problems and in promoting respect for human rights and fundamental freedoms; and (d) be a center for harmonizing the actions of nations in attaining these common ends. UN membership includes approximately 170 nations. UN headquarters are located in New York City. The UN structure includes six principal organs, specialized agencies, major programs, autonomous agencies, committees, subsidiary organs, and approximately a dozen peace-keeping forces. Some of the specialized agencies and other bodies were established before the UN was created.

The six principal UN organs are:

— The General Assembly (composed of all UN member nations)

— Security Council

— Economic and Social Council (ECOSOC)

— Trusteeship Council

— International Court of Justice (seated in The Hague, Netherlands)

— The Secretariat (which provides studies, information, and facilities for UN bodies)

United Nations Commission on International Trade Law

UNCITRAL was established in 1966 to aid in harmonizing and unifying international trade law. The Commission has focused on four principal international areas: (a) sales of goods, (b) payments, (c) commercial arbitration, and (d) legislation pertaining to shipping. The Commission issues publications and sponsors training in international trade law.

United Nations Conference on Environment and Development

UNCED promotes global cooperation between developing and industrialized countries in planning and managing environmentally responsible development in four major areas: (a) poverty and the environment; (b) growth patterns, consumption standards, demographic pressures and the environment; (c) international economic problems; and (d) policies, institutions, and sustainable development. UNCED was established in December 1989; headquarters are in Conches, Switzerland.

United Nations Conference on Trade and Development

UNCTAD was set up in December 1964 as a permanent organ of the UN General Assembly. UNCTAD promotes international trade and seeks to increase trade between developing countries and countries with different social and economic systems. UNCTAD also examines problems of economic development within the context of principles and policies of international trade and seeks to harmonize trade, development, and regional economic policies. Headquarters are in Geneva, Switzerland.

United Nations Development Program

The UNDP provides multilateral grant technical assistance – including expert advice, training, and limited equipment — to developing countries. The Program was established in 1965; headquarters are in New York City.

United Nations Environment Program

The UNEP leads UN environmental activities and assists developing countries in implementing environmentally sound development policies. UNEP produced a worldwide environmental monitoring system to standardize international data. UNEP was established in 1972; headquarters are in Nairobi, Kenya.

United Nations Industrial Development Organization

UNIDO promotes accelerated commercial development in developing countries and encourages industrial cooperation worldwide. As part of its activities, UNIDO identifies promising entrepreneurs in the developing world to the attention of potential partners in industrialized countries through a network of Investment Promotion Services (IPS). IPS offices operate in Austria, China, France, Germany, Italy, Japan, Korea, Russia, Switzerland, and the United States (Washington, D.C.) Established in 1967, UNIDO became a specialized agency on the UN in 1986; headquarters are in Vienna, Austria.

United Nations Regional Commissions

There are five UN commissions which promote economic development as a regional commission for the Educational, Scientific, and Cultural Organization (UNESCO):

— The Economic Commission for Africa (ECA), established April 1958 promotes economic and social development among approximately 50 participating nations; Commission headquarters are in Addis Ababa, Ethiopia.

— The Economic Commission for Europe (ECE), established March 1947, promotes economic cooperation among members; headquarters are in Geneva, Switzerland.

— The Economic Commission for Latin America and the Caribbean (ECLAC — Spanish: Comision Economica para America Latina y el Caribe, CEPAL), originally established as the Economic

Commission for Latin American (ECLA) in February 1948 promotes economic and social development among approximately 40 member states; Commission headquarters are in Santiago, Chile.

— The Economic and Social Commission for Asia and the Pacific (ESCAP), originally established as the Economic Commission for Asia and the Far East (ECAFE) in March 1947; promotes economic development planning and related activities among approximately 38 member nations; Commission headquarters are in Bangkok, Thailand.

— The Economic and Social Commission for Western Asia (ESCWA), originally established as the Economic Commission for Western Asia (ECWA) in August 1973 promotes economic reconstruction and development among fourteen member nations. Commission headquarters are in Baghdad, Iraq.

United States Agricultural Export Development Council

The USAEDC represents the interests of commodity organizations participating in the market development program established by the Foreign Agricultural Service. USAEDC, created in 1954, is composed predominantly of producer and agribusiness oriented non-profit organizations.

United States and Foreign Commercial Service

The State Department's Foreign Commercial Service was transferred to Commerce in April of 1980. This group was merged with Commerce's domestic field operations in 1982, creating the U.S. and Foreign Commercial Service.

United States-Asia Environmental Program

The US-AEP, announced in January 1992, helps U.S. companies compete in expanding Asian markets for sales of environmental products, services, technologies, and know-how. US-AEP, coordinated by AID, links the efforts of U.S. government agencies in a one-stop service.

United States Council for International Business

USCIB is the American affiliate of the International Chamber of Commerce (ICC), the Business and Advisory Council (BIAC) to the Organization for Economic Cooperation and Development, and the International Organization of Employers (IOE). The Council advocates U.S. business positions to the U.S. Government, to United Nations bodies, and to other international organizations. The Council administers the ATA Carnet System, which issues and guarantees documents that allow duty-free, temporary importation of merchandise overseas. The Council was established in 1945; headquarters are in New York City.

United States Customs Service

An agency of the Treasury Department charged with enforcing laws relative to imports.

United States government securities

Debt issues of the U.S. government, as distinguished from government-sponsored agency issues.

United States International Trade Commission

See: International Trade Commission.

United States Price

In the context of dumping investigations, this term refers to the price at which goods are sold in the U.S. compared to their foreign market value. The comparisons are used in the process of determining whether imported merchandise is sold at less than fair value.

United States Trade Representative

The USTR is a cabinet-level official with the rank of Ambassador who advises the President on trade policy. The USTR coordinates the development of U.S. trade policy initiatives; leads U.S. international trade negotiations; and seeks to expand U.S. exports by promoting removal or reduction of foreign trade barriers.

The Office of the USTR was created as the Office of the Special Representative for Trade Negotiations by Executive Order (11075) in January 1963. The Trade Act of 1974 established the Office as an agency of the Executive Office of the President, charged with administering the trade agreements program under the Tariff Act of 1930, the Trade Expansion Act of 1962, and the Trade Act of 1974. Other powers and responsibilities for coordinating trade policy were assigned to the Office by the Trade Act of 1974 and by the President by Executive Order in March 1975, as amended. Reorganization Plan No. 3 of 1979 (implemented by Executive Order in January 1980), charged the Office with responsibility for setting and administering overall trade policy and identified the USTR as the chief representative of the U.S. for all activities of the General Agreement on Tariffs and Trade, for negotiation on trade and commodity issues in the Organization of Economic Cooperation and Development, for negotiations in the United Nations Conference on Trade and Development, and for trade and commodity negotiations in other multilateral institutions and in other bilateral and multilateral negotiations concerning trade as a primary issue.

United States Travel and Tourism Administration

USTTA is an agency in the Commerce Department; it's principal mission is to implement broad tourism policy initiatives for the development of international travel to the U.S. as a stimulus for economic stability.

Unit investment trust

Money invested in a portfolio whose composition is fixed for the life of the fund. Shares in a unit trust are called redeemable trust certificates, and they are sold at a premium to net asset value.

Unit of trading

See: Trading unit.

Unit Price

The price of a selected unit of good or service; e.g., price per ton, per dozen, per box, etc.

Unit Share Investment Trust (USIT)

A unit investment trust comprising one unit of prime and one unit of score.

Unit trust

In the United Kingdom and other foreign markets, an open-end mutual fund.

Universal life

A whole life insurance product whose investment component pays a competitive interest rate rather than the below-market crediting rate.

Universe of securities

A group of stocks having a common feature, such as similar outstanding market capitalization or same product line.

Unleveraged beta

The beta of an unleveraged required return (i.e., no debt) on an investment when the investment is financed entirely by equity.

Unleveraged program

The use of borrowed funds to finance less than 50% of

a purchase of assets. In a leveraged program borrowed funds are used to finance more than 50%.

Unleveraged required return

The required return on an investment when the investment is financed entirely by equity (i.e., no debt).

Unlevered cost of equity

The discount rate appropriate for an investment that it is financed with 100% equity.

Unlimited liability

Full liability for the debt and other obligations of a legal entity. The general partners of a partnership have unlimited liability.

Unlimited marital deduction

An Internal Revenue Service provision that allows an individual to transfer an unlimited amount of assets to a spouse, during life or at death, without incurring federal estate or gift tax.

Unlimited tax bond

A municipal bond secured by the pledge to levy taxes until full repayment at an unlimited rate.

Unlisted security

A security traded in the over-the-counter market that is not listed on an organized exchange.

Unlisted trading

Trading in unlisted securities that occurs on an organized exchange to accommodate members. This practice is not permitted at the NYSE.

Unloading

Selling securities or commodities whose prices are dropping to minimize loss.

Unmargined account

A cash account held at a brokerage firm.

Unmatched book

If the average maturity of a bank's liabilities is shorter than that of its assets, it is said to be running an unmatched book. The term is commonly used with the Euromarket. Also refers to entering into OTC derivatives contracts and not hedging by making trades in the opposite direction to another financial intermediary. In this case, the firm with an unmatched book usually hedges its net market risk with futures and options. Related expressions: Open book and short book.

Unpaid dividend

A dividend declared by the directors of a corporation that has not yet been paid.

Unqualified opinion

An independent auditor's opinion that a company's financial statements comply with accepted accounting procedures. Antithesis of qualified opinion.

Unrealized capital gain/loss

An increase/decrease in the value of a security that is not "real" because the security has not been sold. Once a security is sold by the portfolio manager, the capital gains/losses are "realized" by the fund, and any payment to the shareholder is taxable during the tax year in which the security is sold.

Unseasoned issue

Issue of a security for which there is no existing market. See: Seasoned issue.

Unsecured debt

Debt that does not identify specific assets that the debtholder is entitled to in case of default.

Unsterilized intervention

Foreign exchange market intervention in which the monetary authorities have not insulated their domestic money supplies from the foreign exchange transactions.

Unsystematic risk

Also called the diversifiable risk or residual risk. The risk that is unique to a company such as a strike, the outcome of unfavorable litigation, or a natural catastrophe that can be eliminated through diversification. Related: Systematic risk.

Unwind a trade

Reverse a securities transaction through an offsetting transaction in the market.

Up

Market indication; willingness to go both ways (buy or sell) at the mentioned volume and market. Print; up on the ticker tape, confirming that the trade has been executed.

Up tick

Plus tick.

Upgrading

Raising the quality rating of a security because of new optimism about the prospects of a firm due to tangible or intangible factors. This can increase investor confidence and push up the price of the security.

Upset price

The minimum price at which a seller of property will accept a bid at an auction.

Upside potential

The amount by which analysts or investors expect the price of a security may increase.

Upstairs market

A network of trading desks for the major brokerage firms and institutional investors, which communicate with each other by means of electronic display systems and telephones to facilitate block trades and program trades.

Upstairs order

Used for listed equity securities. Off-floor order.

Upswing

An upward turn in a security's price after a period of falling prices.

Uptick rule

SEC rule that selling short is allowed only on an up tick.

Uptick trade

A transaction that takes place at a higher price than the preceding transaction involving the same security. Related: Tick test rules.

Uruguay Round

Eighth round of multilateral negotiations held under the GATT's auspices. The talks began in Uruguay in September 1986 and concluded successfully in December 1993. The round resulted in a comprehensive agreement liberalizing trade in goods and services that came into force in January 1, 1995.

US

The two-character ISO 3166 country code for UNITED STATES.

U.S. Affiliate

A U.S. affiliate is a U.S. business enterprise in which there is foreign direct investment — that is, in which a single foreign person owns or controls, directly or indirectly, 10 percent or more of its voting securities if the enterprise is incorporated or an equivalent interest if the enterprise is unincorporated. The affiliate is called a U.S. affiliate to denote that the affiliate is located in the U.S. (although it is owned by a foreign person). See: Foreign Person.

Usance

The time allowed for settlement of a draft.

Usance Draft

See: Time Draft.

Usance Letter of Credit

A letter of credit payable at a determined future date after presentation of conforming documents.

U.S.-Canada Free Trade Agreement (CFTA or FTA)

Implemented in January 1989 to eliminate all tariffs on U.S. and Canadian goods by January 1998 and to reduce or eliminate many nontariff barriers.

USD

The ISO 4217 currency code for the USA Dollar.

Useful life

The expected period of time during which a depreciating asset will be productive.

U.S.-Japan Semiconductor Trade Arrangement

See: Semiconductor Trade Arrangement.

U.S. Munitions List

The USML identifies those items or categories of items considered to be defense articles and defense services subject to export control. The USML is similar in coverage to the International Munitions List (IML), but is more restrictive in two ways. First, the USML currently contains some dual-use items that are controlled for national security and foreign policy reasons (such as space-related or encryption-related equipment). Second, the USML contains some nuclear-related items. Under Presidential directive, most dual-use items are to be transferred from the USML to the Commerce Department's dual-use list. State, with the concurrence of Defense, designates which articles will be controlled under the USML. Items on the Munitions List face a stricter control regime and lack the safeguards to protect commercial competitiveness that apply to dual-use items.

US Treasury bill

US government debt with a maturity of less than a year.

US Treasury bond

US government debt with a maturity of more than 10 years.

US Treasury note

US government debt with a maturity of one to 10 years.

U.S. Treasury securities

Interest-bearing obligations if the U.S. government issued by the U.S. Department of the Treasury as a means of borrowing money to meet government expenditures not covered by tax revenues. There are three types of marketable Treasury securities-bills, notes and bonds.

Usual Marketing Requirements

UMR is the amount of a commodity which a P.L. 480 ("Food for Peace") sales agreement requires the recipient country to import on a commercial basis. This amount is normally based on the country's most recent 5-year average of commercial imports of the commodity from countries friendly to the United States.

Usury laws

Laws limiting the amount of interest that can be charged on loans.

Utility

A power company that owns or operates facilities used for the generation, transmission, or distribution of electric energy, which is regulated at state and federal levels.

Utility function

A mathematical expression that assigns a value to all possible choices. In portfolio theory, the utility function expresses the preferences of economic entities with respect to perceived risk and expected return.

Utility revenue bond

A municipal bond issued to finance the construction of public utility services. These bonds are repaid from the operating revenues the project produces after the utility is finished.

Utility value

The welfare a given investor assigns to an investment with a particular expected return and risk.

UY

The two-character ISO 3166 country code for URUGUAY.

UYU

The ISO 4217 currency code for the Uruguay Peso Uruguayo.

UZ

The two-character ISO 3166 country code for UZBEKISTAN.

UZS

The ISO 4217 currency code for the Uzbekistan Sum.

V

Fifth letter of a Nasdaq stock symbol indicate that it is when-issued or when-distributed.

VA

The two-character ISO 3166 country code for HOLY SEE (VATICAN CITY STATE).

Validated Export License

A document issued by the U.S. government authorizing the export of commodities for which written export authorization is required by law. Two types exist: an Individual Validated License (IVL) and a Special License.

Valuation

Determination of the value of a company's stock based on earnings and the market value of assets.

Valuation Clause

The clause in the Marine Policy that contains a fixed basis of valuation agreed upon by the Assured and the Underwriter and which establishes the insured value of the merchandise. The Clause determines the amount payable under any recoverable loss or General Average contribution.

Valuation Opportunity Cost

The potential increase in firm value associated with investments that are for gone due to capital rationing.

Valuation reserve

An allowance to provide for changes in the value of a company's assets, such as depreciation.

Value Added

The difference between the value of goods produced and the cost of materials and services purchased to produce them. It includes wages, interest, rent, and profits. The sum of value added of all sectors of the economy equals GDP.

Value Added Counseling

Valued added counseling is defined as assessing a company's current international business operations and assisting a client in one or more of the following: (a) identifying and selecting the most viable markets; (b) developing an export market strategy; (c) implementing the export market strategy; and (d) increasing market presence.

Value-Added Tax

A European Community (EC) tax assessed on the increased value of goods as they pass from the raw material stage through the production process to final consumption. The tax on processors or merchants is levied on the amount by which they increase the value of items they purchase. The EC charges a tax equivalent to the value added to imports and rebates value-added taxes on exports.

Value additivity principal

When the value of a whole group of assets exactly equals the sum of the values of the individual assets that make up the group of assets. Or, the principle that the net present value of a set of independent projects is just the sum of the net present values of the individual projects.

Value broker

A discount broker whose rates are a percentage of the dollar value of each transaction.

Value date

In the market for Eurodollar deposits and foreign exchange, the delivery date of funds traded. For spot transactions, it is normally on spot transactions two days after a transaction is agreed upon. In the case of a forward foreign exchange trade, it is the future date.

Value dating

When value or credit is given for funds transferred between banks.

Value for Customs Purposes Only

The U.S. Customs Service defines "value for Customs purposes only" as the value submitted on the entry documentation by the importer which may or may not reflect information from the manufacturer but in no way reflects Customs appraisal of the merchandise.

Value investing

In the context of asset management, mutual funds, and hedge funds, the a style of investment that focuses on securities with low price to earnings ratios or low price to book ratios. Some of these securities are deemed cheap and are viewed by manager as having a lot of profit potential.

Value Line investment survey

A proprietary service that ranks stocks for timeliness and safety.

Value manager

A manager who seeks to buy stocks that are at a discount to their "fair value" and to sell them at or in excess of that value. Often a value stock is one with a low price-to-book value ratio. Opposite of to growth stock.

Value Maximization

Increases in owners' wealth achieved by maximizing of the value of a firm's common stock.

Value-at-risk model (VaR)

Procedure for estimating the probability of portfolio losses exceeding some specified proportion based on a statistical analysis of historical market price trends, correlations, and volatilities.

Value stocks

Stocks with low price/book ratios or price/earnings ratios. Historically, value stocks have enjoyed higher average returns than growth stocks (stocks with high price/book or P/E ratios) in a variety of countries.

Value stock fund

A mutual fund that emphasizes stocks of companies whose growth opportunities are generally regarded as subpar by the market. A value stock company often pays regular dividend income to shareholders and sells at relatively low prices in relation to its earnings or book value.

Vancouver Stock Exchange (VSE)

A securities and options exchange in Vancouver, British Columbia, (Canada), specializing in venture capital companies.

Vanilla issue

A security issue that has no unusual features.

VaR

See: Value-at-risk model.

Variable

An element in a model. For example, in the model $RS\&P_{t+1} = a + b\ Tbill_{t} + e_{t}$, where $RS\&P_{t+1}$ is the return on the S&P in month $_{t+1}$ and Tbill is the Tbill return at month $_{t}$, both RS&P and Tbill are "variables" because they change through time; i.e., they are not constant.

Variable annuities

Investment contracts whose issuer pays a periodic amount linked to the investment performance of an underlying portfolio.

Variable cost

A cost that is directly proportional to the volume of output produced. When production is zero, the variable cost is equal to zero.

Variable interest rate

See: Adjustable rate.

Variable Levy

A tariff subject to alterations as world market prices change, the alterations are designed to assure that the import price after payment of the duty will equal a predetermined "gate" price.

Variable life insurance policy

A whole life insurance policy that provides a death benefit dependent on the insured's portfolio market value at the time of death. Typically the company invests premiums in common stocks, so variable life policies are referred to as equity-linked policies.

Variable Plan

A plan in which either the number of shares and/or the price at which they will be issued is not known on the grant date.

Variable-price security

A security that sells at a fluctuating market-determined price stocks and bonds are example.

Variable-rate

A varible-rate agreement, as distinguished from a fixed-rate agreement, calls for an interest rate that may fluctuate over the life of the loan. The rate is often tied to an index that reflects changes in market rates of interest. A fluctuation in the rate causes changes in either the payments or the length of the loan term. Limits are often placed on the degree to which the interest rate or the payments can vary.

Variable-rate CDs

Short-term certificate of deposits that pay interest periodically on roll dates. On each roll date, the coupon on the CD is adjusted to reflect current market rates.

Variable-rate demand note

A note that is payable on demand and bears interest tied to a money market rate.

Variable-rate loan

Loan made at an interest rate that fluctuates depending on a base interest rate, such as the prime rate or LIBOR.

Variable rated demand bond (VRDB)

Floating-rate bond that periodically can be sold back to the issuer.

Variable Ratio Write

An option strategy in which the investor owns 100 shares of the underlying security and writes two call options against it, each option having a different striking price.

Variance

A measure of dispersion of a set of data points around their mean value. The mathematical expectation of the average squared deviations from the mean. The square root of the variance is the standard deviation.

Variance-minimization approach to tracking

An approach to bond indexing that uses historical data to estimate the variance of the tracking error.

Variance rule

Specifies the permitted minimum or maximum quantity of securities that can be delivered to satisfy a TBA trade. For Ginnie Mae, Fannie Mae, and Freddie Mac pass-through securities, the accepted variance is plus or minus 2.499999 % per million of the par value of the TBA quantity.

Variation margin

An additional required deposit to bring an investor's equity account up to the initial margin level when the balance falls below the maintenance margin requirement.

Vault cash

Cash kept on hand in a depository institution's vault to meet day-to-day business needs, such as cashing checks for customers; can be counted as a portion of the institution's required reserves.

VC

The two-character ISO 3166 country code for SAINT VINCENT AND THE GRENADINES.

VE

The two-character ISO 3166 country code for VENEZUELA.

VEB

The ISO 4217 currency code for the Venezuelan Bolivar.

Velda Sue

Stands for Venture Enhancement and Loan Development Administration for Smaller Undercapitalized Enterprises. A federal agency that buys and pools small business loans made by banks, and then issues securities that are bought by large institutional investors.

Velocity

The number of times a dollar is spent, or turns over, in a specific period of time. Velocity affects the amount of economic activity generated by a given money supply.

Vendor

Any person or entity who sells something.

Venture capital

An investment in a start-up business that is perceived to have excellent growth prospects but does not have access to capital markets. Type of financing sought by early-stage companies seeking to grow rapidly.

Venture capital limited partnership

A partnership between a startup company and a brokerage firm or entrepreneurial company that provides capital for the new business in return for stock in the company and a share of the profits.

Vertical acquisition

Buying or taking over a firm in the same industry in which the acquired firm and the acquiring firm represent different steps in the production process.

Vertical analysis

Dividing each expense item in the income statement of a given year by net sales to identify expense items that rise more quickly or more slowly than a change in sales.

Vertical Export Trading Company

An export trading company that integrates a range of functions taking products from suppliers to consumers.

Vertical line charting

A form of technical charting that shows the high, low, and closing prices of a stock or a market on each day on one vertical line with the closing price indicated by a short horizontal mark.

Vertical merger

When one firm acquires another firm that is in the same industry but at another stage in the production cycle. For example, the firm being acquired serves as a supplier to the firm doing the acquiring.

Vertical spread

Simultaneous purchase and sale of two options that differ only in their exercise price. See: Horizontal spread.

Vessel

Every description of watercraft or other artificial contrivance used, or capable of being used, as a means of transportation on water.

Vest

Become applicable or exercisable. A term mainly used on the context of employee stock ownership or option programs. Employees might be given equity in a firm but they must stay with the firm for a number of years before they are entitled to the full equity. This is a vesting provision. It provides incentive for the employee to perform.

Vesting

Nonforfeitable ownership (or partial ownership) by an employee of the retirement account balances or benefits contributed on the employees behalf by an employer. The Tax Reform Act of 1986 established minimum vesting rights for employees based on their years of service—full vesting in five years or 20% vesting per year starting by the end of the third year.

Vesting Schedule

Schedule setting forth when, and to what extent, options become exercisable or restricted stock or stock units are no longer subject to forfeiture (for example, 20% per year over five years).

Veterans Administration (VA) mortgage

A home mortgage loan granted by a lending institution to U.S. veterans and guaranteed by the Veterans Administration.

V formation

A technical chart pattern that follows a letter V form, indicating that the security price has bottomed out, and is now in a bullish trend.

VG

The two-character ISO 3166 country code for VIRGIN ISLANDS, BRITISH.

VI

The two-character ISO 3166 country code for VIRGIN ISLANDS, U.S..

Vienna Convention

Common name for the United Nations Convention on Contracts for the International Sale of Goods. They are a body of law governing the international sale of goods between parties domiciled in member countries.

Vienna Stock Exchange (VSX)

One of the world's oldest exchanges, which accounts for approximately 50% of Austrian stock transactions; the balance are traded OTC.

Vignette

A symbol or pictorial representation of the corporation on a stock certificate. Usually a complicated and artistic design, it is meant to make the counterfeiting of stock certificates as difficult as possible.

Virtual currency option

A new option contract introduced by the PHLX in 1994 that is settled in US dollars rather than in the underlying currency. These options are also called 3-Ds (dollar-denominated delivery).

Visa

Visas are required by many countries for entry of a foreigner. A visa is a stamp in a foreign national's passport issued by a U.S. consular officer which creates a legal presumption that there are no apparent reason to deny entry into the U.S. Regardless of the stamp, the final decision to grant admission is made by an officer of the U.S. Immigration Service at the port of entry.

Visa Waiver

A program of selected countries to eliminate the visa requirement on a test basis.

Visit USA Committee

A committee of U.S. tourism managers located in foreign markets. Visit USA Committees work with USTTA and the U.S. & Foreign Commercial Service in planning and promoting travel to the U.S.

Visible supply

New muni bond issues scheduled to come to market within the next 30 days.

VIX

The implied volatility on the S&P 100 (OEX) option. This volatility is meant to be a forward looking volatility. It is calculated from both calls and puts that are near the money. The VIX is a popular measure of market risk.

VN

The two-character ISO 3166 country code for VIET NAM.

VND

The ISO 4217 currency code for the Vietnamese Dong.

Voluntary Export Restriction

An understanding between trading partners in which the exporting nation, in order to reduce trade friction, agrees to limit its exports of a particular good. Also called voluntary restraint agreement.

Voluntary Restraint Agreement

Informal bilateral or multilateral understandings in which exporters voluntarily limit exports of certain products to a particular country destination in order to avoid economic dislocation in the importing country and the imposition of mandatory import restrictions. These arrangements do not involve an obligation on the part of the importing country to provide "compensation" to the exporting country, as would be the case if the importing country unilaterally imposed equivalent restraints on imports. See Voluntary Export Restriction.

Volatility

A measure of risk based on the standard deviation of the asset return. Volatility is a variable that appears in option pricing formulas, where it denotes the volatility of the underlying asset return from now to the expiration of the option. There are volatility indexes. Such as a scale of 1-9; a higher rating means higher risk.

Volume counting

The SEC dictates how volume is counted. Thus, volume is counted in the same manner on all markets based on the above reporting structure. Any time money changes hands (or any time capital is risked), it must be counted as a trade. Examples: 1) One registered market participant on Nasdaq buys 100 shares into inventory from another registered market participant or from one of its clients. In either case, it is counted as 100 shares. 2) One member firm on the NYSE or Amex buys 100 shares from another member firm. The Specialist matches the order between the two firms and it is counted as 100 shares. 3)The Specialist sells 100 shares from his inventory to a member firm on the NYSE. It is counted as 100 shares. 4) A Market Maker receives an order to buy 100 shares from it's client. It does not have 100 shares in its inventory. It must go buy 100 shares from someone else. It then sells these 100 shares to the client. Thus, there are two trades in this example for a total of 200 shares.

Volume deleted

A note appearing on the consolidated tape when the tape is running behind under heavy trading, meaning that only the stock symbol and price will be shown for trades under 5000 shares.

Volume discount

A reduction in price based on the purchase of a large quantity.

Voluntary accumulation plan

Arrangement allowing shareholders of a mutual fund to purchase shares over a period of time on a regular basis, and in so doing take advantage of dollar cost averaging.

Voluntary bankruptcy

The legal proceeding that follows a petition of bankruptcy.

Voluntary liquidation

Liquidation proceedings that are supported by a company's shareholders.

Voluntary plan

A pension plan supported partially by the employee by pension contributions deducted from each paycheck.

Volatility risk

The risk in the value of options portfolios due to the unpredictable changes in the volatility of the underlying asset.

Voting Instruction Card

The voting card sent to participants in an employee plan giving the trustee of the plan the authority to vote the shares as indicated on a proxy card.

Volume

This is the daily number of shares of a security that change hands between a buyer and a seller.

Voting certificate

Certificates issued by a voting trust to stockholders in exchange for their common stock, which represent all the rights of common stock except voting rights.

Voting rights

The right to vote on matters that are put to a vote of security holders. For example the right to vote for directors.

Voting stock

The shares in a corporation that entitle the shareholder to vote.

Voting trust certificate

A trust in which control of a corporation is given to a few individuals, usually to support reorganization of a corporation without interference.

VPA

Vendor Payment Authorization.

V.R.A.

See Voluntary Restraint Agreement.

VRDB

See: Variable-rated demand bond.

VU

The two-character ISO 3166 country code for VANUATU.

VUV

The ISO 4217 currency code for the Vanuatu Vatu.

VWAP

The volume-weighted average price.

VXN

The implied volatility on the Nasdaq 100 (NPX) option. This volatility is meant to be a forward looking volatility. It is calculated from both calls and puts that are near the money.

W

Fifth letter of a Nasdaq stock symbol indicating that this particular stock is a warrant.

W-8

Certificate of Foreign Status form required by the IRS to tell the payer, transfer agent, broker or other middleman that an employee is a nonresident alien or foreign entity that is not subject to U.S. tax reporting or backup withholding rules.

W-9

Request for Taxpayer Identification Number and Certification form required by the IRS to furnish the payer, transfer agent, broker or other middleman with an employee's social security or taxpayer identification number, in order that the employee not be subject to backup withholding because of under-reporting of interest and dividends on his or her tax return.

W-9

A form used to certify a shareholder's social security or tax identification number as true and correct, in order to avoid federal tax withholding.

WACC

See: Weighted average cost of capital.

Wage assignment

A loan agreement provision allowing the lender to deduct payments from an employee's wages in case of default.

Wage-push inflation

Inflation caused by skyrocketing wages.

Waiting period

Time during which the Securities and Exchange Commission (SEC) studies a firm's registration statement. During this time the firm may distribute a preliminary prospectus.

Waiver of premium

A provision in an insurance policy that allows payment of insurance premiums to be permanently or temporarily stopped in the event the policyholder becomes incapacitated.

Walk away

To take and maintain a position in a stock after going to the floor to consummate a trade. Antithesis of trade me out, buy them back.

Wall Street

Generic term for the securities industry firms that buy, sell, and underwrite securities.

Wall Street analyst

Related: Sell-side analyst

Wallflower

Stock that has fallen out of favor with investors; stock that tends to have a low P/E (price-to-earnings ratio).

Wallpaper

A security with no monetary value.

Wanted for cash

A statement displayed on market tickers indicating that a bidder will pay cash for same-day settlement of a block of a specified security.

War babies

Slang term for the stocks and bonds of corporations in the defense industry.

War chest

Cash kept aside for a takeover or for defense against a takeover bid.

Separate insurance coverage against loss or damage due to acts of war (including objects left over from previous wars).

Warehouse Receipt

A receipt issued by a warehouse listing goods received for storage. A charge assessed by a pier or dock owner for handling incoming or outgoing cargo.

Warehouse-To-Warehouse Clause

The clause in the Cargo Policy that defines when coverage commences and terminates. It is the intent of the policy to attach at the time the goods leave the warehouse of origin named in the Policy, and to continue while the goods are in due course of transit until delivered to the warehouse of destination named in the Policy, where it terminates.

Warehousing

The interim holding period from the time of the closing of a loan to its subsequent marketing to capital market investors.

Warrant

A security entitling the holder to buy a proportionate amount of stock at some specified future date at a specified price, usually one higher than current market price. Warrants are traded as securities whose price reflects the value of the underlying stock. Corporations often bundle warrants with another class of security to enhance the marketability of the other class. Warrants are like call options, but with much longer time spans-sometimes years. And, warrants are offered by corporations, while exchange-traded call options are not issued by firms.

Warranty

A guarantee by a seller to a buyer that if a product requires repair or remedy of a problem within a certain period after its purchase, the seller will repair the problem at no cost to the buyer.

War Risks

Those risks related to two (or more) belligerents engaging in hostilities, whether or not there has been a formal declaration of war. Such risks are excluded by the F.C.&S. (Free of Capture and Seizure) Warranty, but may be covered by a separate War Risk Policy, at an additional premium.

War Risk Insurance

Warsaw Stock Exchange

The major securities market of Poland.

Wash

Gains equal losses.

Wash sale

Purchase and sale of a security either simultaneously or within a short period of time, often in order to recognize a tax loss without altering one's position. See: Tax selling.

Wasting asset

An asset that has a limited life and thus decreases in value (depreciates) over time. Also applies to consumed assets, such as oil or gas, and termed "depletion."

Watch list

A list of securities selected for special surveillance by a brokerage, exchange, or regulatory organization; firms on the list are often takeover targets, companies planning to issue new securities, or stocks showing unusual activity.

Watered stock

A stock representing ownership in a corporation that is worth less than the actual invested capital, resulting in problems of low liquidity, inadequate return on investment, and low market value.

Waybill

A document (that looks like a bill of lading) issued by a carrier that describes the goods to be transported and that details the shipping particulars. Waybills are issued by both air carriers (air waybills) and ship lines (sea waybills). They merely indicate that the stated goods were received by the carrier for transport, they do not convey title.

Weak dollar

A depreciated dollar with respect to other currencies, meaning that more dollars are needed to buy a unit of foreign currency. Antithesis of strong dollar.

Weak-form efficiency

A pricing theory that the price of a security reflects the past price and trading history of the security.

Theory implies that security prices follow a random walk. Related: Semistrong-form efficiency, strong-form efficiency.

Weak market

A market with few buyers and many sellers and a declining trend in prices.

Webb-Pomerene Association

Associations engaged in exporting that combine the products of similar producers for overseas sales. These associations have partial exemption from U.S. anti-trust laws but may not engage in import, domestic or third country trade or combine to export services.

WEBS

See: World Equity Benchmark Series.

Wedge

A chart pattern composed of two converging lines connecting peaks and troughs. In the case of falling wedges, the pattern indicates temporary interruptions of upward price rallies. In the case of rising wedges, indicates interruptions of a falling price trend.

Weekend effect

The common recurrent low or negative average return from Friday to Monday in the stock market.

Weight

Either Gross Weight, Net Weight, or Tare Weight.

Weighted Average

An average that reflects the underlying quantities of its components. For example, whereas the average per capita GDP of European countries would treat Greece and Germany equally, the weighted-average per capita GDP would refkect Germany's greater population.

Weighted average cost of capital (WACC)

Expected return on a portfolio of all a firm's securities. Used as a hurdle rate for capital investment. Often the weighted average of the cost of equity and the cost of debt The weights are determined by the relative proportions of equity and debt in a firm's capital structure.

Weighted average Coupon

The weighted average of the gross interest rates of mortgages underlying a pool as of the pool issue date; the balance of each mortgage is used as the weighting factor.

Weighted average life

See: Average life

Weighted average maturity

The weighted average maturity of an MBS is the weighted average of the remaining terms to maturity of the mortgages underlying the collateral pool at the date issue, using as the weighting factor the balance of each of the mortgages as of the issue date.

Weighted average portfolio yield

The weighted average of the yield of all the bonds in a portfolio.

Weighted average remaining maturity

The average remaining term of the mortgages underlying a MBS.

Well-diversified portfolio

A portfolio that includes a variety of securities so that the weight of any security is small. The risk of a well-diversified portfolio closely approximates the systematic risk of the overall market, and the unsystematic risk of each security has been diversified out of the portfolio.

West Africa Economic Community (CEAO)

CEAO (French: Communauté Economique de l'Afrique de l'Ouest), created in 1974, includes: Benin, Burkina Faso, Cote d'Ivoire, Mali, Mauritania, Niger, and Senegal. (Togo has observer status). The CEAO operates as a free trade area for agricultural products and raw materials and as a preferential trading area for approved industrial products, with a regional cooperation tax (TCR) replacing import duties and encouraging trade among members. A Community fund (FOSIDEC) promotes private lender Community participation in advancement of the Community's least developed nations (Burkina Faso, Mali, Mauritania, and Niger). CEAO envisions eventual creation of a customs union and coordination of fiscal policies. Community headquarters are in Ouagadougou, Burkina Faso.

West African Clearing House (WACH)

WACH (French: Chambre de Coôpération de l'Afrique de l'Ouest, CCAO) provides settlement of payments services among central bank and other monetary authorities in West Africa. WACH was established in 1975 (began operations in 1976); headquarters are in Freetown, Sierra Leone. Membership includes the Central Bank of West African States (representing Benin, Burkina Faso, Côte d'Ivoire, Mali, Niger, Senegal, and Togo) as well as The Gambia, Ghana, Guinea, Guinea-Bissau, Liberia, Mauritania, Nigeria, and Sierra Leone.

West African Development Bank (WADB)

The West African Development Bank, WADB, (French: Banque Quest-Africaine de D,veloppement, BOAD) promotes regional economic development and integration in West Africa. The Bank was established in 1973 (began operations in 1976); headquarters are in Lom,, Togo. WADB members include: Benin, Burkina Faso, Côte d'Ivoire, Mali, Niger, Senegal, and Togo.

West African Monetary Union (WAMU)

WAMU (French: Union Monétaire Quest Africaine, UMOA) began operation in 1963 and was revised in 1973. The Union comprises seven French-speaking African countries: Benin, Burkina Faso, Cote d'Ivoire, Mali, Niger, Senegal, and Togo which share a: (a) central bank (Banque Centrale des Etats de l'Afrique de l'Ouest) which coordinates the Union's monetary and credit policies; (b) common currency (CFA Franc) which is freely convertible into the French Franc at a fixed parity; and (c) a common regional development bank, the West African Development Bank. WAMU headquarters are in Daka, Senegal.

West Africa Rice Development Association (WARDA)

WARDA conducts research on rice improvement in mangrove swamps, inland swamps, upland conditions, and irrigated conditions. The Association is one of several centers associated with the Consultative Group on International Agricultural Research. WARDA was established in 1970; headquarters are in Bouake, Côte d'Ivoire. Members include 16 West African countries: Benin, Burkina Faso, Chad, Côte d'Ivoire, Gambia, Ghana, Guinea, Guinea-Bissau, Liberia, Mali, Mauritania, Niger, Nigeria, Senegal, Sierra Leone, and Togo. See Consultative Group on International Agricultural Research.

Western European Union (WEU)

The WEU was created in October 1954 (began operations in May 1955) to promote mutual defense and progressive political unification of its members. The Union, which serves interests between those furthered by the European Economic Community and the North Atlantic Treaty Organization, has faced the need to change and has become focused on three missions: humanitarian aid, peacekeeping, and crisis management and some peace enforcement considerations. Membership, which included Belgium, France, Germany, Italy, Luxembourg, the Netherlands, Portugal, Spain, the United Kingdom, has been increasing toward approximately 40 nations as a result of negotiations on membership or associate status with Greece, Turkey, Norway, Iceland, Denmark, and Ireland. WEU headquarters moved from London, England to Brussels, Belgium in December 1992.

WF

The two-character ISO 3166 country code for WALLIS AND FUTUNA.

Wharfage

A charge assessed by a pier or dock owner for handling incoming or outgoing cargo.

When distributed

When issued.

When issued (W.I.)

Refers to a transaction made conditionally, because a security, although authorized, has not yet been issued. Treasury securities, new issues of stocks and bonds, stocks that have split, and in-merger situations after the time the proxy has become effective but before completion are all traded on a when-issued basis. With ice.

Whipsawed

Buying stocks just before prices fall and selling stocks just before prices rise in a volatile market, often as the result of misleading signals.

Whisper number or forecast

An unofficial earnings estimate of a company given to clients by a security analyst if there is more optimism or pessimism about earnings than shown in the published number. These are often found on the Internet.

Whisper stock

A stock rumored to be the target of a takeover bid, drawing speculators who hope to make a profit after the takeover is completed.

Whistle blower

A person who has knowledge of fraudulent activities inside a firm or government agency, who is protected from the employer's retribution by federal law.

White knight

A friendly potential acquirer sought out by a target firm that is threatened by a less welcome suitor.

White Noise

The audio equivalent of Brownian motion. Sounds that are unrelated and sound like a hiss. The video equivalent of white noise is "snow" in television reception.

White sheets

Lists of prices published by the National Quotation Bureau for Market Makers.

White-shoe firm

Broker-dealer firms that disdain practices such as hostile takeovers.

White squire

White knight who buys less than a majority interest.

White's rating

A rating of municipal securities, that uses market factors rather than credit considerations to find appropriate yields.

Whitemail

Sale of a large amount of stock by a company that is the target of a takeover bid to a friendly party at below-market prices, so that the raider is forced to buy more of highly priced shares to accomplish the takeover.

Whole life insurance

A contract with both insurance and investment components: (1) It pays off a stated amount upon the death of the insured, and (2) it accumulates a cash value that the policyholder can redeem or borrow against.

Whole loan

A term that distinguishes an investment representing an original mortgage loan from a loan representing a participation with one or more lenders.

Wholesale mortgage banking

The purchasing of loans originated by others, for the acquisition of the servicing rights.

Wholesaler

An underwriter or a broker-dealer who trades with other broker-dealers, rather than with the retail investor.

Wholly owned subsidiary

A subsidiary whose parent company owns virtually 100% of its common stock.

Whoops

A nickname for the Washington Public Power Supply System, which in the 1970s raised billions of dollars through municipal bond offerings, the projects that never materialized. WPPSS defaulted on the payments to bondholders.

WI

See: When issued.

Wi WI

Come from when issued. Treasury bills trade on a WI basis between the day they are auctioned and the day settlement is made. Bills traded before they are auctioned are said to be traded WI WI

Wide opening

Abnormally wide spread between the bid and asked prices of a security at the opening of a trading session.

Widow-and-orphan stock

A stock paying high dividends with a low beta and noncyclical business, that is an extremely safe investment.

Wiener Börse (Austrian Stock Exchange)

Established in 1771, the major securities market of Austria.

Wild card option

The right of the seller of a Treasury bond futures contract to give notice of intent to deliver at or before 8:00 p.m. Chicago time after the closing of the exchange (3:15 p.m. Chicago time) when the futures settlement price has been fixed. Related: Timing option.

Williams Act

Federal legislation enacted in 1968 (and now constituting Rules 13d and 14d of the Security Exchange Act of 1934) that imposes requirements with respect to public tender offers.

Wilshire indexes

Widely followed performance measurement indexes measuring performance of all U.S.-headquartered equity securities with readily available price data, created by Wilshire Associates, Inc.

Windfall profit

A sudden unexpected profit uncontrolled by the profiting party.

Window

A brokerage firm's cashier department, where delivery of securities and settlement of transactions take place.

Window contract

A guaranteed investment contract purchased with deposits over some future designated time period (the "window"), usually between 3 and 12 months. All deposits made are guaranteed the same credit rating. Related: Bullet contract.

Window dressing

Trading activity near the end of a quarter or fiscal year that is designed to improve the appearance of a portfolio to be presented to clients or shareholders. For example, a portfolio manager may sell losing positions so as to display only positions that have gained in value.

Winnipeg Commodity Exchange

Canada's only agricultural futures and options exchange, located in Manitoba.

Winner's curse

Problem faced by uninformed bidders. For example, in an initial public offering uninformed participants are likely to receive larger allotments of issues that informed participants know are overpriced.

Wire house

A firm operating a private wire to its own branch offices or to other firms, commission houses, or brokerage houses.

Wire room

A department within a brokerage firm that receives customers' orders and transmits the orders to the exchange floor or the firm's trading department.

Wire transfer

Electronic transfer of funds; usually involves large dollar payments.

With Average

A marine insurance term meaning that a shipment is protected from partial damage whenever the damage exceeds 3 percent (or some other percentage). If the ship is involved in a major catastrophe, such as a collision, fire or stranding, the minimum percentage requirement is waived and the insurance company pays for all of the damage. See Marine Cargo Insurance.

With dividend

Purchase of shares that entitle the buyer to the forthcoming dividend. Related: Ex-dividend.

Withdrawal plan

Agreement that a mutual fund will disburse automatic periodic redemptions to the investor.

Withholding

Used in the context of securities, the illegal practice of a public offering participant keeping some shares in a private account or with a family member, employee, or dealer to profit from the higher market price of a hot issue. Used in the context of taxes, the withholding by an employer of a certain amount of an employee's income in order to cover the employee's tax liability. Also used to refer to the withholding by corporations and financial institutions of a flat 10% of interest and dividend payments due to security holders.

Withholding tax

A tax levied by a country of source on income paid, usually on dividends remitted to the home country of the firm operating in a foreign country.

With ice

When issued.

With rights

Shares sold accompanied by entitlement the buyer to buy additional shares in the company's rights issue.

Without

Indicates a one-way market if 70 were bid in the market and there was no offer, the quote would be "70 bid without.".

Without Reserve

A term indicating that a shipper's agent or representative is empowered to make definitive decisions and adjustments abroad without approval of the group or individual represented.

With Particular Average (WPA)

See: With Average.

Without recourse

Giving the lender no right to seek payment or seize assets in the event of nonpayment from anyone other than the party specified in the debt contract (such as a special-purpose entity).

Without Recourse Financing

Financing in which the right of recourse to the party receiving funds is forfeited to the party advancing funds. This may be evidenced by conditions added to the endorsement of a draft being sold by an exporter in order to protect the exporter, if the instrument is not paid at maturity by the original obligor.

Woody

Slang to describe a market moving strongly upward, as in, "This market has a woody."

Working

Attempting to complete the remaining part of a trade, by finding either buyers or sellers for the rest.

Working away

Transacting with another broker/dealer.

Working capital

Defined as the difference between current assets and current liabilities (excluding short-term debt). Current assets may or may not include cash and cash equivalents, depending on the company.

Working capital management

The deployment of current assets and current liabilities so as to maximize short-term liquidity.

Working capital ratio

Working capital expressed as a percentage of sales.

Working control

Control of a corporation by a shareholder or shareholders having less than 51% voting interest because of the wide dispersion of share ownership.

Working order

Standing order in the marketplace, through which a broker bids or offers to fill the order in a series of lots at opportune times in hopes of obtaining the best price.

Workout

Informal repayment or loan forgiveness arrangement between a borrower and creditors.

Workout market

Market indicating prices at which it is believed a security can be bought or sold within a reasonable length of time.

Workout period

Realignment of a temporarily misaligned yield relationship that sometimes occurs in fixed income markets.

World Administrative Radio Conference (WARC)

WARC refers to the conferences convened regularly by the United Nations' International Telecommunications Union (ITU) to allocate and regulate radio frequencies for the purposes of television and radio broadcasting, telephone data communications, navigation, maritime and aeronautical communication, and satellite broadcasting.

World Agricultural Outlook Board (WAOB)

The WAOB acts as the focal point for U.S. economic intelligence related to domestic and international food and agriculture. The Board coordinates and clears all commodity and aggregate agricultural and food-related data used to develop outlook and situation material within the Department of Agriculture. WAOB was established in 1977.

World Bank

The World Bank is an integrated group of international institutions which provides financial and technical assistance to developing countries. The World Bank includes the International Bank for Reconstruction and Development and the International Development Association. World Bank affiliates, legally and financially separate, include the International Center for Settlement of Investment Disputes, the International Finance Corporation, and the Multilateral Investment Guarantee Agency. World Bank headquarters are in Washington, D.C.

World Confederation of Labor (WCL)

The WCL represents the cultural, economic, political, and social interests of millions of workers in Africa, the Americas, Asia, Europe, and the Middle East. The Confederation was founded in 1920 as the International Federation of Christian Trade Unions (IFCTU .. not to be confused with ICFTU, the International Confederation of Free Trade Unions); headquarters are in Brussels, Belgium.

World Equity Benchmark Series (WEBS)

The World Equity Benchmark Series are similar to SPDRs. WEBS trade on the AMEX, and track the Morgan Stanley Capital International (MSCI) country indexes. WEBS are available for: Australia, Austria, Belgium, Canada, France, Germany, Hong Kong, Italy, Japan, Malaysia Free, Mexico, the Netherlands, Singapore, Spain, Sweden, Switzerland, and the United Kingdom.

World Federation of Development Financing Institutions (WFDFI)

WFDFI (Spanish: Federacion Mundial de Instituciones Financieras de Desarollo, WFDFI) promotes improved technical operations of, and coordination among, worldwide development banking activities. Federation members include development financing institutions. The Federation was established in 1979; headquarters are in Madrid, Spain.

World Food Council (WFC)

The WFC is a UN body which was created in December 1974 to help eliminate hunger and malnutrition. The Council monitors world food production, consumption, and trade patterns. The Council provides a forum for international discussion and assistance on ways of improving food production in developing countries and in increasing world food security. WFC headquarters are in Rome, Italy.

World Food Program (WFP)

The WFP, created in 1963, is a United Nations program with headquarters in Rome, Italy. WFP administers the International Emergency Food Reserve and supports projects which incease agricultural production, nutrition, and social and economic development in developing countries.

World Health Organization (WHO)

The WHO (French: Organisation Mondiale de la Sant,, OMS) is a specialized agency of the United Nations which sets standards for the quality control of drugs, vaccines, and other substances affecting health. WHO was established in July 1946; headquarters are in Geneva, Switzerland. See Codex Alimentarius Commission.

World Intellectual Property Organization (WIPO)

WIPO (French: Organisation Mondiale de la Propri,t, Intellectuelle, OMPI) promotes protection of intellectual property around the world through cooperation among states, and administers various "Unions," each founded on a multilateral treaty and dealing with the legal and administrative aspects of intellectual property. The Organization was established in 1967 (came into force in 1970), and became a specialized agency of the United Nations in December 1974; headquarters are in Geneva, Switzerland.

World investible wealth

The part of world wealth that is traded and is therefore accessible to investors.

World Meteorological Organization (WMO)

Originally established under another name in 1875, the WMO was reconstituted and renamed in 1951. The WMO facilitates worldwide cooperation in establishing a network for meteorological, hydrological, and geophysical observations, for exchanging meteorological and related information, and for promoting standardization in meteorological measurements. Organization headquarters are in Geneva, Switzerland.

World Tourism Organization (WTO)

The WTO, associated with the United Nations, is an intergovernmental technical body dealing with all aspects of tourism. The Organization promotes and develops tourism as a means of contributing to economic development, international understanding, peace, and prosperity. The WTO provides a world clearing house for the collection, analysis, and dissemination of technical tourism information and it offers national tourism administrations and organizations a means for multilateral approaches to international discussions and negotiations on tourism policy and practice. The Organization was established in November 1974; headquarters are in Madrid, Spain.

World Trade Organization (WTO)

Provisions to establish the WTO were reached in the Uruguay Round of the General Agreement on Tariffs and Trade (GATT). The WTO is scheduled to be established no later than 1997 as an international organization of comparable stature to the World Bank and the International Monetary Fund. The Organization is expected to facilitate implementation of trade agreements reached in the Uruguay Round by bringing them under one institutional umbrella, requiring full participation of all countries in one new trading system, and providing a permanent forum to discuss new issues facing the international trading system. The WTO system will be available only to countries which: (a) are contracting parties to the GATT, (b) agree to adhere to all of the Uruguay Round agreements, and (c) submit schedules of market access commitments for industrial goods, agricultural goods, and services.

World Traders Data Reports (WTDR)

WTDR is an International Trade Administration fee-based service which provides a confidential background report on a specific foreign firm, prepared by commercial officers overseas. WTDRs provide information about the type of organization, year established, relative size, number of employees, general reputation, territory covered, language preferred, product lines handled, principal owners, financial references, and trade references. WTDRs include narrative information about the reliability of the foreign firm.

Wrap account

An investment consulting relationship for management of a client's funds by one or more money managers, that bills all fees and commissions in one comprehensive fee charged quarterly.

Wraparound

A financing device that permits an existing loan to be refinanced and new money to be advanced at an interest rate between the rate charged on the old loan and the current market interest rate. The creditor combines or "wraps" the remainder of the old loan with the new loan at the intermediate rate.

Wraparound annuity

An investment that allows the annuitant the choice of underlying investments tax-deferred.

Wraparound mortgage

A second mortgage that leaves the original mortgage in force. The wraparound mortgage is held by the lending institution as security for the total mortgage debt. The borrower makes payments on both loans to the wraparound lender, which in turn makes payments on the original senior mortgage.

Wrinkle

A feature of a new product or security intended to entice a buyer.

Write

Sell an option. Applies to derivative products.

Write-down

Reducing the book value of an asset if its is overstated compared to current market values.

Write-off

Charging an asset amount to expense or loss, such as through the use of depreciation and amortization of assets.

Write out

The procedure used when a specialist makes a trade

involving his own inventory, on one hand, and a floor broker's order, on the other. The broker must first complete the trade with the specialist, who then transacts a separate trade with the customer.

Writer

The seller of an option, usually an individual, bank, or company that issues the option and consequently has the obligation to sell the asset (if a call) or to buy the asset (if a put) on which the option is written if the option buyer exercises the option.

Writing cash-secured puts

An option strategy to avoid using a margin account. Instead of depositing margin with a broker, a put writer can deposit a cash balance equal to the option exercise price, and can avoid additional margin calls.

Writing naked

See: Naked option

Writing puts to acquire stock

Selling a put option at an exercise price that would represent a good investment by an option writer who believes a stock's value will fall, so that the writer cannot lose. If the stock price unexpectedly goes up, the option will not be exercised and the writer is at least ahead the amount of the premium received. If the stock loses value, as expected, the option will be exercised, and the writer has the stock at what he had earlier decided was originally a good buy, and he has the premium income in addition.

Written-down value

The book value of an asset after allowing for depreciation and amortization.

WS

The two-character ISO 3166 country code for SAMOA.

WST

Western Samoa Tala currency

WTO

See World Trade Organiation

W-type bottom

A double bottom pattern in a price history that looks like the letter W. See: Technical analysis.

X

Fifth letter of a Nasdaq stock symbol indicating that listing is a mutual fund.

XAF

The ISO 4217 currency code for the CFA Franc.

XBA

The ISO 4217 currency code for the European Composite Unit (EURCO).

XBB

The ISO 4217 currency code for the European Monetary Unit (EMU).

XCD

The ISO 4217 currency code for the East Caribbean Dollar.

XDR

The ISO 4217 currency code for the Special Drawing Rights (SDR).

XEU

The ISO 4217 currency code for the European currency Unit (ECU).

XMI

Applies to derivative products. Quotron symbol for the Major Market Index (MMI).

XOF

The ISO 4217 currency code for the CFA Franc.

XPF

The ISO 4217 currency code for the CFP Franc.

X or XD

Symbol that indicating that stock is trading ex-dividend, with no dividend.

XR

Symbol indicating that a stock is trading ex-rights, with no rights attached.

XW

Symbol indicating that a stock is trading ex-warrants, with no warrants attached.

Y

Fifth letter of a Nasdaq stock symbol specifying that it is an ADR

Yankee bonds

Foreign bonds denominated in U.S. dollars and issued in the United States by foreign banks and corporations. These bonds are usually registered with the SEC. Such as, bonds issued by originators with roots in Japan are called Samurai bonds.

Yankee CD

A CD issued in the domestic market, typically New York, by a branch of a foreign bank.

Yankee market

The foreign market in the United States.

Yard

Slang for one billion currency units. Used particularly in currency trading, e.g., for Japanese yen since one billion yen equals approximately US$10 million. It is clearer to say, "I'm a buyer of a yard of yen," than to say, "I'm a buyer of a billion yen," which could be misheard as "I'm a buyer of a million yen."

YE

The two-character ISO 3166 country code for YEMEN.

Year-end dividend

A special dividend declared at the end of a fiscal year that usually represents distribution of higher-than-expected company profits.

Year-to-date (YTD)

The period beginning at the start of the calendar year up to the current date.

Yellow sheets

Sheets published by the National Quotation Bureau that detail bid and ask prices, plus those firms that are making a market in over-the-counter corporate bonds.

Yen bond

Any bond denominated in Japanese yen currency.

YER

The ISO 4217 currency code for the Yemen Rial.

Yield

The percentage rate of return paid on a stock in the form of dividends, or the effective rate of interest paid on a bond or note.

Yield advantage

The advantage gained by purchasing convertible securities instead of common stock, which equals the difference between the rates of return of the convertible security and the common shares.

Yield burning

A municipal bond financing method. Underwriters in advance refundings add large markups on US Treasury bonds bought and held in escrow to compensate investors while waiting for repayment of old bonds after issuance of the new bonds. Since bond prices and yields move in opposite directions, when the bonds are marked up, they "burn down" the yield, which may violate federal tax rules and diminishes tax revenues.

Yield curb

Applies mainly to convertible securities. Difference in current yield between the convertible and the underlying common.

Yield curve

The graphic depiction of the relationship between the yield on bonds of the same credit quality but different maturities. Related: Term structure of interest rates. Harvey (1991) finds that the inversions of the yield curve (short-term rates greater than long term rates) have preceded the last five US recessions. The yield curve can accurately forecast the turning points of the business cycle.

Yield curve option-pricing models

Models that can incorporate different volatility assumptions along the yield curve, such as the Black-Derman-Toy model. Also called arbitrage-free option-pricing models.

Yield curve strategies

Investments that position a portfolio to capitalize on expected changes in the shape of the Treasury yield curve.

Yield differential/pickup

Mainly applies to convertible securities. Graph showing the term structure of interest rates by plotting the yield of all bonds of the same quality with maturities ranging from the shortest to the longest available.

Yield equivalence

The interest rate at which a tax-exempt bond and a taxable security of similar quality give the investor the same rate of return.

Yield ratio

The quotient of two bond yields.

Yield spread

The difference in yield between different security issues usually securities of different credit quality.

Yield spread strategies

Investments that position a portfolio to capitalize on expected changes in yield spreads between sectors of the bond market.

Yield to average life

A yield calculation in which bonds are retired routinely during the life of the issue. Since the issuer buys its own bonds on the open market because of sinking fund requirements, if the bonds are trading below par, this action provides automatic price support for these bonds and they will usually trade on a yield to average life basis.

Yield to call

The percentage rate of a bond or note if the investor buys and holds the security until the call date. This yield is valid only if the security is called prior to maturity. Generally bonds are callable over several years and normally are called at a slight premium. The calculation of yield to call is based on coupon rate, length of time to call, and market price.

Yield to maturity

The percentage rate of return paid on a bond, note, or other fixed income security if the investor buys and holds it to its maturity date. The calculation for YTM is based on the coupon rate, length of time to maturity, and market price. It assumes that coupon interest paid over the life of the bond will be reinvested at the same rate.

Yield to warrant call

Applies mainly to convertible securities. Effective yield of usable or synthetic convertible bonds determined against the first date at which the warrants can be called.

Yield to warrant expiration

Applies mainly to convertible securities. Effective yield of usable convertible bonds determined by the expiration date of the applicable warrants.

Yield to worst

The bond yield computed by using the lower of either the yield to maturity or the yield to call on every possible call date.

Yo-yo stock

A highly volatile stock that moves up and down like a yo-yo.

YT

The two-character ISO 3166 country code for MAYOTTE.

YU

The two-character ISO 3166 country code for YUGOSLAVIA.

YUM

The ISO 4217 currency code for the Yugoslavia New Dinar.

Z

Z

Fifth letter of a Nasdaq stock symbol indicating that listing is a fifth class of preferred stock, a stub, a certificate representing a limited partnership interest, foreign preferred when issued, or a second class of warrants.

ZA

The two-character ISO 3166 country code for SOUTH AFRICA.

Zabara

Applies mainly to international equities. Japanese securities transactions conducted on the principal of auction, i.e., (1) price priority in which the selling (buying) order with the lowest (highest) price takes precedence over other orders, and (2) time priority in that an earlier order takes precedence over other orders at the same price.

Zaibatsu

Large family-owned conglomerates that controlled much of the economy of Japan prior to World War II.

Zangger Committee

The Zangger Committee of the Nonproliferation Treaty Exporters examines controls enacted pursuant to the Nuclear Nonproliferation Treaty by refining the list of items requiring nuclear safeguards. The Zangger Committee consists of 23 Nuclear Non-Proliferation Treaty (NPT) nuclear supplier nations which includes all nuclear weapons states except France and China. Through a series of consultations in the early 1970's, the countries of the Zangger Committee compiled a "trigger list" of nuclear materials and equipment. The shipment of any item on the list to a non-nuclear weapons state "triggers" the requirement of International Atomic Energy Agency (IAEA) safeguards. Since the Zangger Committee is associated with the NPT, its members are obligated to treat all non-nuclear weapons parties to the treaty alike. For fear of discrediting the NPT, the Zangger countries cannot target strict nuclear controls toward certain nations with questionable proliferation credentials; the NPT binds them to assist non-nuclear weapons states with peaceful atomic energy projects.

ZAR

The ISO 4217 currency code for the South Africa Rand.

ZBA

See: Zero balance account.

Z bond

A bond on which interest accrues but is not currently paid to the investor but rather is added to the principal balance of the Z bond and becoming payable upon satisfaction of all prior bond classes.

Zero-balance account (ZBA)

A checking account in which zero balance is maintained by transfers of funds from a master account in an amount only large enough to cover checks presented.

Zero-base budgeting (ZBB)

Budgeting method that disregards the previous year's budget in setting a new budget, since circumstances may have changed. Each and every expense must be justified in this system.

Zero-beta portfolio

A portfolio constructed to have zero systematic risk, similar to the risk-free asset, that is, having a beta of zero.

Zero-bracket amount

The standard deduction portion of income which is not taxed for taxpayers choosing not to itemize deductions.

Zero-coupon bond

A bond in which no periodic coupon is paid over the life of the contract. Instead, both the principal and the interest are paid at the maturity date.

Zero-coupon convertible security

A zero-coupon bond convertible into the common stock of the issuing company after the stock reaches a certain price, using a put option inherent in the security. Also refers to zero-coupon bonds, which are convertible into an interest bearing bond at a certain time before maturity.

Zero-investment portfolio

A portfolio of zero net value established by buying and shorting component securities, usually in the context of an arbitrage strategy.

Zero-minus tick

Sale that takes place at the same price as the previous sale, but at a lower price than the last different price. Antithesis of zero-plus tick.

Zero-one integer programming

An analytical method that can be used to determine the solution to a capital rationing problem.

Zero prepayment assumption

The assumption of payment of scheduled principal and interest with no payments.

Zero-plus tick

Used for listed equity securities. Transaction at the same price as the preceding trade, but higher than the preceding trade at a different price. Antithesis of zero-minus tick. See: Short sale.

Zero-sum game

A type of game wherein one player can gain only at the expense of another player.

Zero uptick

Related: Tick-test rules.

ZM

The two-character ISO 3166 country code for ZAMBIA.

ZMK

The ISO 4217 currency code for Zambian Kwacha .

Zombies

Companies that continue operation while they await merger or closure, even though they are insolvent and bankrupt.

Zone d'Echanges Préférentiels pour les Etats de l'Afrique de l'Est et de l'Afrique Australe

See Preferential Trade Area for Eastern and Southern African States.

ZRN

The ISO 4217 currency code for the Zaire New Zaire.

Z score

Statistical measure that quantifies the distance (measured in standard deviations) a data point is from the mean of a data set. Separately, Z score is the output from a credit-strength test that gauges the likelihood of bankruptcy.

ZW

The two-character ISO 3166 country code for ZIMBABWE.

ZWD

The ISO 4217 currency code for the Zimbabwe Dollar.